PH PRESTWICK HOUSE, INC.
*"Everything for the English Classroom!"*

# SATIRE:
## FROM
## HORACE
## TO
## YESTERDAY'S
## COMIC STRIPS

WRITTEN BY: JAMES SCOTT

EDITED BY:
ELIZABETH OSBORNE AND DOUGLAS GRUDZINA

ISBN 978-1-58049-112-9

# TABLE OF CONTENTS

# Note to Students

This collection of cartoons, poems, stories, and essays is designed to give you a broad view of satire and make you more aware of satire in the mass media. Editorial comics, song parodies, and television shows like *Saturday Night Live* are actually part of a tradition that goes back to early in recorded history. Satire has been used as a form of social and political expression for thousands of years; as long as even a single person sees flaws that need to be pointed out in society or institutions, it will remain an important tool.

# CHAPTER I
## WHAT IS SATIRE?

## Why Create Satire?

Making fun of other people comes naturally to most of us. Putting someone down verbally, after all, is safer than getting into a physical fight, and words can hit someone as hard as a fist. Since human beings could talk, they've been using insults to put each other down or build themselves up—maybe some of both. But there is a careful and complex language of ridicule—a person who does not know where to stop may earn powerful enemies or lose valuable friends.

The genre of literature whose purpose is to ridicule is called SATIRE. Although the ancient Greeks wrote plays with satirical elements, the first true satires were written by Romans. They were poems composed of several different elements (the word SATURA means "mixed dish" or "medley").

More than two thousand years later, satire is all around us. Political cartoons, sketch comedy shows, and song parodies all qualify as satire, but it can be difficult to say why. After all, a picture in a newspaper depicting a celebrity as an animal is very different from a poem dealing with the greed of a typical Roman businessman. And how can the insults that a developing rap sensation throws at an established star be related to the insults that 19th-century sensation Lord Byron unleashed on his competitors?

If you keep in mind every time—and every way—you've ever made fun of someone or heard someone get put down, you won't have much difficulty understanding the heart of satire. Though it comes in many complex forms (broadside, caricature, invective, lampoon, parody, travesty) and tones (from gentle and affectionate to out-and-out furious to ice-cold and deadly) and can be aimed at any number of targets, its purpose is always to ridicule.

# Satire, Politics, and Society

By its very nature, satire is controversial and offensive. No person or group likes to have its attitudes, beliefs, or behaviors ridiculed. During the eight years of Bill Clinton's presidency, for instance, moderate-to-liberal-Democrats had a tendency to criticize the nation's conservative press (including newspaper cartoonists) for unfair treatment of the President. Ironically, during George W. Bush's presidency, conservative Republicans criticized the liberal press for *its* unfair treatment of the President.

When it comes to satire, concepts of fairness and truth seem to depend on who is playing the satirist and who is the target. In fact, the political implications of satire are so strong that tyrannical and totalitarian regimes throughout history have censored, exiled, and even executed satirists.

The Roman poet Juvenal, for instance, was exiled from Rome for criticizing a friend of the Emperor Domitian. When the next emperor, Hadrian, came to power, Juvenal was allowed to return.

Voltaire (Francois-Marie Arouet) was also the target of political opposition for his satires. In 1716, he was arrested and exiled from Paris for five months. From 1717 to 1718, he was imprisoned in the Bastille for his attacks on the French government and the Catholic Church.

The history of literature in Czarist Russia and the Soviet Union includes a long list of satiric playwrights and novelists who were sentenced to exile or forced to stop writing.

Even in twenty-first century United States, satire provokes outrage. In October of 2004, a major US retail chain simply refused to offer its customers two books it considered offensive.

The First Amendment to the Constitution of the United States protects the satirist's right to free speech, as long as the satire does not deteriorate into the punishable crimes of *slander* or *libel*. Slander is the act of intentionally telling lies that injure another person's reputation. Libel is the writing and publishing of these damaging lies.

Outside of these two crimes, which are extremely difficult to prove, any kind of satire is permissible in the United States. Even the President is a potential target of a satirist's wit.

# Decoding Satire on Paper:
## Tone, Target, and Background Knowledge

Listening to someone tell a story, you may sometimes think to yourself, "Does she mean that?" You automatically look for clues in the way a person talks and moves, as well as what you know about the person already, to figure out how serious the person is.

Analyzing written work can be trickier. Instead of hearing a writer speak, you have to "hear" the emotions imbedded within the writing. Taken together, these emotions make up the TONE of a piece. A poem, for example, may be nasty and sarcastic, mock-enthusiastic, or pompous and high-flown in tone.

In the example below (from Voltaire's *Candide*), the tone is reasonable and factual.

> The next day he [Candide] did his exercise a little less
> badly, and he received but twenty blows. The day
> following they gave him only ten, and he was regarded
> by his comrades as a fast learner.

What the author actually says, however, is ridiculous, and this leads us to the next tool we need to master in the study of satire: IRONY. When an author says something that he or she clearly does not believe, or takes on a tone that is at odds with what he or she is saying, we say that irony is being used.

Irony appears in the following lines from the *Canterbury Tales*. The poet Geoffrey Chaucer describes a monk, a supposedly holy man whose job is to care for the poor and sick:

> It wasn't fitting, by his faculty,
> To have with unwell lepers acquaintance.
> It is not honest, it may not advance,
> For to have dealings with such lepers rude—
> Only the rich and sellers of fine foods.

Both we and Chaucer know that the monk is not doing what he should, but Chaucer presents the monk's case in a straightforward manner.

Irony can sneak into a piece of writing when you are not looking; suddenly, you realize, the joke is on you. This is what makes satire a dangerous game. As the famous satirist Jonathan Swift said, "Satire is a sort of glass, wherein beholders do generally discover everybody's face but their own." Miss the joke, and you may be seriously offended by something (like Swift's own shocking suggestion on page 95) not meant literally. Worse, you may actually see the point, and find that it is you being mocked. (If you happen to be a ruling power, this can be dangerous to your authority, so you might make things dangerous for any satirist who mocks you.)

When reading a satire, then, you should identify the TARGET as best you can. In some satires, this will be easy—Voltaire's *Candide*, for instance (page 72), is directed at a particular philosopher, while Mark Twain states plainly in the essay on page 103 that his target is the writing of James Fenimore Cooper and the critics who have praised Cooper. Most often the target is some larger group behaving in a way the satirist finds incorrect. Greedy priests, deceptive government officials, smug middle-class couples, literary critics who value fancy words above truly well-designed poetry—all are involved in trends that satirists feel should be corrected. In fact, some satirists deal with the even larger issues of universal human shortcomings. Horace, for instance, who was one of the first satirists, asks why men are never happy with what they have. Surely this question will be as relevant tomorrow afternoon as in 14 B.C.E., and any one of us can picture himself or herself as its target.

Finally, knowing some background information about a satirist can help you determine the tone and target of a work. If you know that Jonathan Swift was a passionate defender of the Irish, for instance, you will know that his "Modest Proposal" is not really anti-Irish; you can see that although its tone is cool and practical, it is actually bitterly sarcastic.

Tone, target, and background knowledge are rarely separate; knowing about each helps you understand the others.

# Important Terms

**Broadside, Invective:** These are terms for a direct attack. Both the Roman poet Juvenal and the American columnist H.L. Mencken state their opinions without irony or sarcasm; it easy to figure out what they are trying to say.

**Caricature, Exaggeration:** Satirists often exaggerate or distort something in order to emphasize it. The most well-known forms of *caricature* are drawings of well-known figures with certain features greatly exaggerated. President Jimmy Carter, for instance, was famous for his wide, enthusiastic smile and strong Southern accent; cartoonists always played up his smile when they drew him. Similarly, comedians imitating President Carter on television always used double-wide smiles and ridiculous Southern accents.

**Irony:** A condition that arises when there is a difference between what someone means to say and what he/she actually says. An author might be deliberately ironic, claiming something that he/she clearly does not believe. Or a character, like Sinclair Lewis' George Babbitt might say things that the author does not believe. A satirist may emphasize irony by repeating, or having a character repeat, these kinds of things. Robert Southey does so in the poem on page 35.

**Social Satire:** A specific genre of satire that plays on the difference between what a character or group says and does. Look at Sinclair's Babbitt, who talks the talk of a "man's man," disdaining fancy clothes, but actually spends most of his time vainly admiring his own image. Chaucer's religious pilgrims, too, claim to follow Christ as a model, but cheat, lie, and commit adultery.

**Parody, Travesty, Send-up, Spoof:** These are terms used for literature that mocks another form or style of literature. *Don Quixote* is a parody of medieval Spanish romances; it uses many of the traits of these works, but makes them seem silly by applying them to an old man and a drunken peasant. *Mock-epic* is a very specific form of parody that ridicules grand poetry of the *epic* genre. Byron's *Don Juan* is an example of a mock-epic.

# CHAPTER II

## SATIRE IN THE CONTEMPORARY MEDIA

## Cartoons

Much of today's satire appears in the pages of the newspaper, especially in the editorial cartoons. As is true for all satire, cartoons and comic strips are funny only if you recognize the target of the satire and are not offended if it is your view that is being satirized.

Take a look at the cartoon below and read the questions that follow. Then, answer the questions that accompany the remaining cartoons.

DOONESBURY © 2003 G.B. TRUDEAU. REPRINTED WITH PERMISSION OF UNIVERSAL PRESS SYNDICATE. ALL RIGHTS RESERVED.

11

1. **What is the target of this satire?**

   *In this cartoon, the target of the satire is American society's
   tendency to fill up children's leisure schedules with "worthwhile"
   activities, limiting time for honest relaxation, reflection, and
   creative play.*

2. **What is the satirist's view?**

   *The satirist, Gary Trudeau, ultimately sides with the mother who
   allowed her daughter to play freely by the pond all summer and build a
   tree fort.*

3. **How can you tell the satirist's view?**

   *The biggest clue to Trudeau's view is the fact that the character
   representing the social trend is herself unfulfilled by the schedule she
   planned for her daughter and sympathetic to her child's level of stress
   and exhaustion. Her final statement, too, is ironic: allowing a child to
   play freely instead of working nonstop is clearly not child abuse.*

4. **Who might be offended by this cartoon?**

   *Parents who  strictly schedule their children's lives, like the mother in
   this cartoon, may not see any humor at all in the strip. Or they may
   be offended, feeling that their parenting is being attacked.*

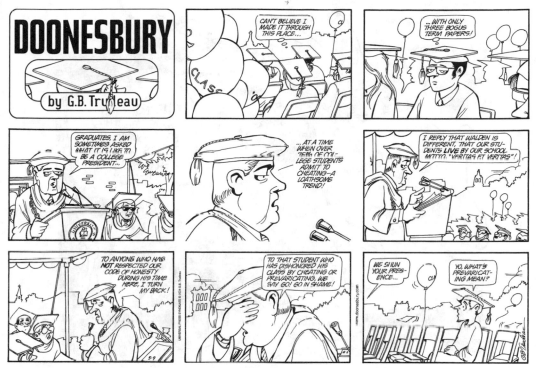

1. What is this cartoon mocking? Is it making fun of a specific individual or a trend in society?

2. "Veritas et Veritas" is a spoof on traditional college mottoes; it means "Truth and Truth." Why does the cartoonist put this detail into the cartoon?

3. What is implied by the final panel in the cartoon?

4. What is the cartoonist's point?

1.  Who is the person holding the egg?

2.  What purpose does the Easter Bunny serve in the cartoon? Does the
    cartoon seem as humorous if you do not know who the Easter
    Bunny is?

3.  What is the illustrator satirizing?

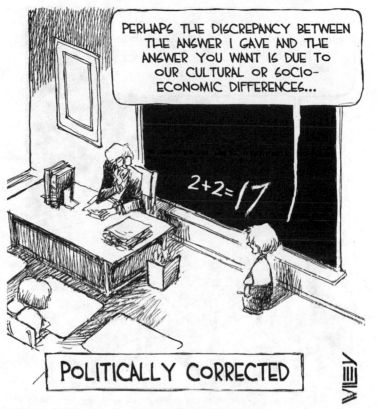

In the 1970s and 1980s, a movement to recognize the validity of different groups—racial, gender and cultural, for instance—began. People who felt that this trend was going too far began to use the term *political correctness* to describe what they saw as a ridiculous exaggeration of the "special qualities" of each group. They claimed that groups often relied on political correctness to win special favors or exception from penalty.

1.  Why does the boy at the chalkboard try to take advantage of political correctness?

2.  What does the author think about political correctness?

3.  What is the author suggesting about contemporary education?

1.  What is absurd or unusual in this cartoon?

2.  What is the cartoonist mocking?

3.  What are some other ways the cartoonist might express this same idea?

**Assignment:**

     Examine several recent newspapers and magazine and find five different satirical cartoons or comic strips. Who or what seems to be the most frequent target of the satire? What seems to be the prevailing attitude toward this person or issue?

# Television and Movies

Television is an excellent medium for satire. In the 1990s and first years after 2000, sketch comedy shows like *Saturday Night Live,* the *Dave Chappelle Show*, and *Mad TV*, along with animated series like *The PJs, The Simpsons,* and *Family Guy* all targeted America's culture and politics.

Movies sometimes deal with current events, but usually cannot respond to things as immediately as television can. As a result, satire in movies is often directed at trends that have developed over a long period of time. After horror films gained popularity in the late 1990s, for instance, a series of movies making fun of the genre came out. The first, called *Scary Movie*, mocked the predictable plots and stereotypical characters in the horror films.

Because *Scary Movie* imitates the films it is ridiculing, it is called a PARODY or SPOOF.

**Assignment:**

Find a satire on television. After watching several episodes, write an informal essay about it. Identify and discuss the targets of the satire and the methods the show uses to ridicule these targets.

Some possible subjects of this essay are listed below.

*South Park*
*Mad TV*
*The PJs*
*Saturday Night Live*
*The Simpsons*
*The Daily Show*

# CHAPTER III
## SATIRE IN POETRY

## Roman Satire

When you first see a comedy sketch on television or a political cartoon in the newspaper, you can usually pick out pretty quickly what person or practice the satirist is mocking. The excerpts of Roman satires you will read here, however, may confuse you. Just remember that Horace and Juvenal are pointing out flaws that they see in society. Do not worry about names and terms that are unfamiliar; focus on extracting the main idea of each excerpt and thinking about whether you agree with it or not.

*Note that these selections from Horace and Juvenal are loose translations.*

## Horace

Horace (65-8 B.C.) remains one of the most skilled satirists. He loves to write about literature; what makes good poetry, why some bad writers love reciting their own verse, and whether a satirist is justified in criticizing others through writing are all favorite subjects.

Horace also, as you will see in the second excerpt, has some critical words to say about the political system in Rome. Roman men who wanted to advance had to seek out the favor of a powerful *patron* (financial supporter), and Horace is not pleased by the flattery and dishonesty that some men use to keep this favor. On the other hand, he is not against the idea of patronage; he often writes fondly of his own patron, Maecenas.

## from Satire I

How comes it, say, Maecenas, if you can,
That none will live like a contented man
Where choice or chance directs, but each must praise
The folk who pass through life by other ways?
"Those lucky merchants!" cries the soldier stout,
When years of toil have well-nigh worn him out:
What says the merchant, tossing o'er the brine?
"Yon soldier's lot is happier, sure, than mine:
One short, sharp shock, and presto! all is done:
Death in an instant comes, or victory's won."
The lawyer lauds the farmer, when a knock
Disturbs his sleep at crowing of the cock:
The farmer, dragged to town on business, swears
That only citizens are free from cares.

## Questions:

1.  What are the four classes of men Horace describes, and why is each one dissatisfied?

2.  What is Horace's main point in this excerpt?

3.  What human quality is Horace mocking?

4.  What is the tone of his mockery? Is it gentle or harsh?

In Satire XVIII, Horace describes two extremes of human behavior. Look at the following excerpt and see if you can identify them.

### from Satire XVIII

You'd blush, good Lollius,[1] if I judge you right,
To mix the parts of friend and parasite.
'Twixt parasite and friend a gulf is placed,
Wide as between the wanton and the chaste;
Yet think not flattery friendship's only curse:
A different vice there is, perhaps a worse,
A brutal boorishness, which fain[2] would win
Regard by unbrushed teeth and close-shorn skin,
Yet all the while is anxious to be thought
Pure independence, acting as it ought.
Between these faults 'tis Virtue's place to stand,
At distance from the extreme on either hand.
The flatterer by profession, whom you see
At every feast among the lowest three,
Hangs on his patron's looks, takes up each word
Which, dropped by chance, might else expire unheard,
Like schoolboys echoing what their masters say
In sing-song drawl, or Gnatho[3] in the play:
While your blunt fellow battles for a straw,
As though he'd knock you down or take the law:
"How now, good sir? you mean my word to doubt?
When I once think a thing, I mayn't speak out?
Though living on your terms were living twice,
Instead of once, 'twere dear at such a price."
And what's the question that brings on these fits?—
Does Dolichos[4] or Castor make more hits?
Or, starting for Brundisium,[5] will it pay
To take the Appian or Minucian[6] way?

[1]Lollius–friend of Horace
[2]fain–eagerly, gladly
[3]Gnatho–name of a low-ranking flatterer in a Roman play
[4]Dolichos and Castor–two minor gladiators
[5]Brundisium–resort town outside Rome
[6]Appian/Minucian way–two roads of about equal length

**Questions:**

1.  What are the two attitudes towards patronage that Horace satirizes?

2.  Where, according to Horace, is true Virtue in relation to the extremes?

3.  Does the blunt man get upset over serious matters only? Give an example of a question that might make him outraged.


**Discussion/Essay Question:**

Describe someone you know who has been the first or second kind of person Horace describes.

# Juvenal

A century after Horace, Juvenal (Decimus Iunius Iuvenalis) wrote satires that depicted his fellow Romans less gently. He perfected the art of *invective*—bitter and harsh attacks on people he saw as greedy, calculating, and obscene.

Look at Juvenal's views on the difficulties faced by poets in the following excerpt.

### from Satire VII

Nor, indeed, can the Muses'[1] song be sung by sad poverty,
because of which, night, and day, the body wastes away;
Horace is well-fed when he shouts, "Euhoe!"[2]
What place is there for talent, unless your breast heaves with only
poetry, and, borne along by the inspiration of Apollo and Dionysus,[3]
doesn't let in various other worries? A great mind
—not one terrified at the thought of even buying a cheap bedspread—
is required to look at the chariots and horses and battle lines of the gods
and the way the Fury mixed up poor Turnus.
If Vergil[4] had lacked a slave boy and tolerable lodging,
every snake would have fallen from the demoness' hair,
and her solemn trumpet would have sighed noiselessly.

[1]Muses–nine goddesses who each represent one of the arts; poets often called
    upon the Muses to inspire them at the beginning of poems
[2]"Euhoe"–a traditional joyful cry of festival poetry
[3] Apollo and Dionysus–gods who inspire poets
[4]Vergil–a contemporary of Horace and one of the greatest Western poets. In
    Vergil's epic *Aeneid*, a young warrior called Turnus is visited by one of
    the Furies, terrible goddesses of vengeance and destruction.

**Questions:**

1.　What is the main idea of this passage?

2.　Does Juvenal seem to be addressing anyone in particular? Who might his intended audience be?

3.　What image does Juvenal use to back up his point about poverty and poetry?

**Essay Question:**

The poem from which this excerpt comes describes the miserable working and living condition of poets and teachers in Juvenal's day. Write your own satire describing the difficulties of being a teacher or an artist today.

# Geoffrey Chaucer

Formal satire was not widely written in the Middle Ages, although English poet Geoffrey Chaucer (1340-1400) wrote verse that contains satirical elements. In his *Canterbury Tales*, he describes each member of a party of religious pilgrims, then has each tell a story.

The Friar, one such pilgrim, is part of a *mendicant* order (begging) of priests. He has taken a vow to live in poverty, as Christ did, and survive only on the charity that people give him. He is supposed to take care of the poor and sick as he travels through towns and cities. As a holy man, he is also celibate; he is not allowed to marry or be involved with women.

Below you will read a description of him by the narrator, who is traveling with the pilgrims.

from the General Prologue of the *Canterbury Tales*

### The Friar

A friar there was, a wanton[1] and a merry,
A limiter[2]—quite dignified he was.
In all the orders four is none who knows
So much of friendly talk and fair language.
He had arranged full many a marriage
Of young women and girls at his own cost.
Unto his order he was a noble post.
Full well beloved and familiar was he
With franklins[3] everywhere in his country,
And also worthy women of the town;
For he had power of confession
As said himself, more than did a curate,[4]
For of his order he was licentiate.[5]

---

[1]wanton—joyful; also, loving pleasure too much
[2]limiter—friar given a license to beg
[3]franklins—property owners
[4]curate—priest
[5]licentiate—holding special authority to hear confession

Very sweetly heard he confession
And pleasant also was his absolution:
He was an easy man to give penance
Wherever he knew he'd get a good pittance.[6]
For when a man to poor order has given
It is a sign that he has been well shriven.[7]
Since if man gave, the friar dared to vaunt.[8]
He knew that man was truly repentant;
For many a man so hard is in his heart,
He may not weep, although it sorely smarts.
Therefore instead of weeping and good prayers
Men may donate their silver to the poor freres.[9]
His cap-tip was all stuffed full of good knives
And pins that he could hand out to fair wives.
And certainly he had a merry note:
Well could he sing and play upon a rote.[10]
Of story-songs he bore outright the prize.
His neck was white as is the fleur-de-lys.[11]
Also he strong was as a champion.
He knew the taverns well in every town
And every hosteller[12] and tappester[13]
Better than any leper or beggar;
For unto such a worthy man as he
It wasn't fitting, by his faculty,
To have with unwell lepers acquaintance.
It is not honest, it may not advance,
For to have dealings with such lepers rude—
Only the rich and sellers of fine foods.
And he, wherever profit should arise
Was courteous and humble in his ways.
There was no man nowhere so virtuous.
He was the most skilled beggar in his house;
For though a widow didn't have a shoe,

[6]pittance—donation
[7]shriven—given confession
[8]vaunt—assert
[9]freres—brothers; fellow clergymen
[10]rote—fiddle
[11]fleur-de-lys—white iris that was the symbol of the kings of France
[12]hosteller–hotel owner
[13]tappester—barmaid

So pleasant was his "in principio,"[14]
Yet would he have a farthing[15] 'fore he went.
His purchase was much better than his rent.
And rage he could, as was right for a whelp.
In love-days therefore could he give much help,
For there he was not like a cloisterer[16]
With threadbare coat, as is a poor scholar,
But he was like a master or a pope.
Of double-worsted[17] was his semi-cope,[18]
That rounded as a bell out of the press.
Somewhat he lisped, out of wantonness,
To make his English sweet upon the tongue,
And in his harping, when that he had sung,
His eyes did twinkle in his head aright,
As all the stars do in the frosty night.
This worthy limiter was called Huberd.

[14]"in principio"—"in the beginning"; first words of the Old Testament
[15]farthing—coin
[16]cloisterer—clergyman who lives in a *cloister*, a secluded area set aside
for prayer
[17]double-worsted—fine knit
[18]semi-cope—short coat

**Questions:**

1. How does the Friar measure up to the ideals by which he is supposed to live? How does he feel about each of the following? Give an example for each of your answers.
   - poverty
   - sympathy for the sick
   - celibacy

2. IRONY is the condition that arises when what a character says is different from what an audience knows to be true. Does the character of the narrator in this passage say things that he, or perhaps Chaucer, does not really believe? How can you tell?

3. Why are some of the Friar's skills not really something for him to boast about?

**Discussion Questions:**

a. Is there a modern class of people who might be satirized in the same way? Do they claim to care about or help people? How do you know they are lying?

b. How is this material different from the passages you read by Horace and Juvenal?

# Neoclassical Satire

In the 18<sup>th</sup> century, writers like Alexander Pope (1688-1744) and Jonathan Swift (1667-1745) looked to classical sources—especially the poems of Horace and Juvenal—when they sat down to write. This period, therefore, is called the *neoclassical* period.

## Jonathan Swift

Swift was born into an English family in Ireland, and throughout his life, was a defender of the Irish. In 1713, he became Dean of Saint Patrick's Cathedral in Dublin.

The following poem describes a typical London rainstorm; the places mentioned in the last six lines are in one area of London.

### A Description of a City Shower

| | |
|---|---|
| Careful observers may foretell the hour, | 1 |
| (By sure prognostics,[1]) when to dread a shower. | |
| While rain depends, the pensive cat gives o'er | |
| Her frolics, and pursues her tail no more. | |
| Returning home at night, you'll find the sink | |
| Strike your offended sense with double stink. | |
| If you be wise, then, go not far to dine: | |
| You'll spend in coach-hire[2] more than save in wine. | |
| A coming shower your shooting corns presage, | |
| Old a-ches throb, your hollow tooth will rage; | 10 |
| Sauntering in coffeehouse is Dulman[3] seen; | |
| He damns the climate, and complains of spleen.[4] | |
| Meanwhile the South, rising with dabbled wings, | |
| A sable[5] cloud athwart the welkin[6] flings, | |

[1]prognostics–methods of predicting the future
[2]coach-hire–cab fare
[3]Dulman–generic name for a Londoner (what does it sound like?)
[4]spleen–irritability
[5]sable–black
[6]welkin–sky

That swill'd more liquor than it could contain,
And, like a drunkard, gives it up again.
Brisk Susan whips her linen from the rope,
While the first drizzling shower is borne aslope;
Such is that sprinkling which some careless quean
Flirts on you from her mop, but not so clean:          20
You fly, invoke the gods; then, turning, stop
To rail;[7] she singing, still whirls on her mop.
Not yet the dust had shunn'd the unequal strife,
But, aided by the wind, fought still for life,
And wafted with its foe by violent gust,
'Twas doubtful which was rain, and which was dust.
Ah! where must needy poet seek for aid,
When dust and rain at once his coat invade?
Sole coat! where dust, cemented by the rain,
Erects the nap,[8] and leaves a cloudy stain!          30
Now in contiguous drops the flood comes down,
Threatening with deluge this devoted town.
To shops in crowds the daggled[9] females fly,
Pretend to cheapen goods, but nothing buy.
The Templar spruce,[10] while every spout's abroach,[11]
Stays till 'tis fair, yet seems to call a coach.
The tuck'd-up sempstress[12] walks with hasty strides,
While streams run down her oil'd umbrella's sides.
Here various kinds, by various fortunes led,
Commence acquaintance underneath a shed.          40
Triumphant Tories, and desponding Whigs,[13]

---

[7]rail–complain; rant
[8]nap–fuzzy surface
[9]daggled–dirtied
[10]Templar spruce–London lawyers practiced at the Inns of Court, in a building that
    was once the Temple of St. James Church, and so were called *Templars*. A *spruce*
    is a well-dressed man. This man, then, is a well-groomed lawyer–perhaps even
    a little dainty and effeminate.
[11]abroach–opened to let liquid out
[12]sempstress–seamstress
[13]Tories/Whigs–the two main political parties in England in Swift's time. In 1710,
    Queen Anne had switched her allegiance from Whigs to Tories, shifting the
    balance of power in England.

Forget their feuds, and join to save their wigs.
Box'd in a chair the beau impatient sits,
While spouts run clattering o'er the roof by fits,
And ever and anon with frightful din
The leather sounds; he trembles from within.
So when Troy[14] chairmen bore the wooden steed,[15]
Pregnant with Greeks impatient to be freed,
(Those bully Greeks, who, as the moderns do,
Instead of paying chairmen, ran them through,)          50
Laocoon[16] struck the outside with his spear,
And each imprison'd hero quaked for fear.
Now from all parts the swelling kennels flow,
And bear their trophies with them as they go:
Filth of all hues and odour, seem to tell
What street they sail'd from, by their sight and smell.
They, as each torrent drives with rapid force,
From Smithfield[17] to St. Pulchre's[18] shape their course,
And in huge confluence join'd at Snowhill[19] ridge,
Fall from the conduit prone to Holborn[20] bridge.          60
Sweeping from butchers' stalls, dung, guts, and blood,
Drown'd puppies, stinking sprats,[21] all drench'd in mud,
Dead cats, and turnip-tops, come tumbling down the flood.

[14]Troy—country in Asia Minor where the Trojan War was fought
[15]steed—horse. According to legend, the Greeks tricked the Trojans by pretending
    to depart Troy, leaving behind a huge wooden horse; the horse was actually
    hollow and filled with Greek soldiers, who emerged and destroyed the city
    once the horse had been brought inside the gates.
[16]Laocoon—Trojan priest who suspected the horse and tried to reveal that it was
    hollow.
[17]Smithfield—site of the city's main meat marker
[18]St. Pulchre's—the church of St. Sepulchre's-without-Newgate, in northeast London
[19]Snowhill—a stop near St. Pulchre's
[20]Holborn—the district in which St. Pulchre's and Snowhill are located. Site of the
    Inns of Court (the main legal complex of London) as well as Newgate prison.
[21]sprats—herrings

## Questions:

1. Poets of Swift's time frequently use words that seem especially fancy because they are old and rare; this kind of language is called archaic. In line 14, Swift seems to elevate the tone of the poem by using archaic language, but what image does he bring up immediately afterwards? What effect does this have?

2. What comparison does Swift use for the ordinary young man sitting inside his carriage, shaking with fear as the rain hits from outside? Why do you think he does this?

3. Some of Swift's contemporaries were fond of using three rhyming lines at the end of a poem to provide special emphasis. How does Swift use a concluding triplet here?

4. What seems to be the poet's view of human society?

## Discussion/Essay Question:

Write a satire about a storm in your own town or city. What kinds of things would float past you?

# Alexander Pope

One of Swift's friends was Alexander Pope, a brilliant literary critic and translator of classic works (including those of Horace). Pope's *Essay on Criticism*, a long poem dealing with the mental errors made by critics and writers, was published when he was just twenty-three.

In the following excerpt from the *Essay on Criticism*, Pope compares two kinds of literary critics.

Some to conceit[1] alone their taste confine,
And glittering thoughts struck out at every line;
Pleased with a work where nothing's just or fit;
One glaring chaos and wild heap of wit.
Poets, like painters, thus, unskilled to trace
The naked nature and the living grace,
With gold and jewels cover every part,
And hide with ornaments their want of art.
True wit is nature to advantage dressed;
What oft was thought, but ne'er so well expressed;
Something, whose truth convinced at sight we find
That gives us back the image of our mind.
As shades more sweetly recommend the light,
So modest plainness sets off sprightly wit
For works may have more wit than does them good,
As bodies perish through excess of blood.

Others for language all their care express,
And value books, as women men, for dress.
Their praise is still—"the style is excellent,"
The sense they humbly take upon content.
Words are like leaves, and where they most abound
Much fruit of sense beneath is rarely found.
False eloquence, like the prismatic[2] glass.
Its gaudy colors spreads on every place,

[1]conceit–clever ideas
[2]prismatic glass–a prism, which breaks up light into different colors

The face of nature we no more survey.
All glares alike without distinction gay:
But true expression, like the unchanging sun,
Clears and improves whate'er it shines upon;
It gilds[3] all objects, but it alters none.

[3]gilds–covers with gold

## Questions:

1.  What are the two kinds of critics Pope ridicules? What does each value?

2.  How is Pope's writing like that of Horace (found on pages 20-21)?

3.  How does Pope define "true wit"?

## Activity:

Write a brief poem in the style of Pope that criticizes two kinds of musicians, artists, actors, or writers. What problems does each group have? Be sure to provide examples.

# Romantic Period

Beginning around the end of the 1700s, poets began to experiment with new forms, trying to go beyond the strict rules of the neoclassicists. William Wordsworth (1770-1850) was one of the leaders of this rebellion. With his friend, the poet Samuel Taylor Coleridge (1772-1834), he researched English and Scottish ballads—simple folk songs—and wrote poetry in the ballad style.

Also popular were works based on romances—story cycles about legendary figures. These stories were often highly emotional, focusing on the intense feelings and tragic deaths of the heroes or heroines. We now use the term Romantic to describe the literature and philosophy of the early 19th century.

Robert Southey (1774-1843) was a contemporary of Wordsworth. In the ballad below, he imagines a conversation between relatives who live at Blenheim, in modern-day Germany. A war fought there in 1704 was responsible for the deaths of 42,000 men.

### After Blenheim

It was a summer evening;
Old Kaspar's work was done,
And he before his cottage door
Was sitting in the sun.
And by him sported on the green
His little grandchild Wilhelmine.

She saw her brother Peterkin
Roll something large and round
Which he beside the rivulet
In playing there had found;
He came to ask what he had found
That was so large and smooth and round.

Old Kaspar took it from the boy,
Who stood expectant by;
And then the old man shook his head,

And with a natural sigh
"Tis some poor fellow's skull," said he,
"Who fell in the great victory."

"I find them in the garden,
For there's many here about;
And often when I go to plow
The plowshare turns them out.
For many thousand men," said he,
"Were slain in that great victory."

"Now tell us what 'twas all about,"
Young Peterkin he cries;
And little Wilhemine looks up
With wonder-waiting eyes;
"Now tell us all about the war,
And what they fought each other for?"

"It was the English," Kaspar cried,
"Who put the French to rout;
But what they fought each other for
I could not well make out.
But everybody said," quoth he,
"That 'twas a famous victory.

"My father lived at Blenheim then,
Yon little stream hard by;
They burned his dwelling to the ground,
And he was forced to fly:
So with his wife and child he fled,
Nor had he where to rest his head.

"With fire and sword the country round
Was wasted far and wide,
And many a childing mother then
And new-born baby died:
But things like that, you know, must be
At every famous victory.

"They say it was a shocking sight
After the field was won;
For many thousand bodies here
Lay rotting in the sun;
But things like that, you know, must be
After a famous victory.

"Great praise the Duke of Marlboro won
And our good Prince Eugene";
—"Why, 'twas a very wicked thing!"
Said little Wilhelmine;
"Nay...nay...my little girl," quoth he,
"It was a famous victory!"

"And everybody praised the Duke
Who this great fight did win."
—"But what good came *of* it at last?"
Quoth little Peterkin:—
"Why, that I cannot tell," said he,
"But 'twas a famous victory."

**Questions:**

1. What kind of attitude is targeted in this satire?

2. Why does Southey have Kaspar repeat one line several times? Why is the line ironic?

3. What do you think Southey's opinion of war is? How can you tell?

# George Gordon, Lord Byron

Byron (1788-1824) was a figure as famous for his outrageous life as for his poetry. He wrote during the Romantic period, and much of his work deals with passion and beauty, two favorite Romantic subjects. However, he also rebelled against some of the trends of his own time. One of his favorite poets, for instance, was the neoclassicist Alexander Pope, whom some Romantic poets denounced.

In 1807, in response to criticism of one of his earlier works, Byron lashes out with a long poem called *English Bards and Scotch Reviewers*. In it, he deals not only with his critics, but with literary trends and poets he dislikes.

**from *English Bards and Scotch Reviewers***

When Vice triumphant holds her sov'reign sway,
Obey'd by all who nought[1] beside obey;
When Folly, frequent harbinger[2] of crime,
Bedecks her cap with bells of every Clime;
When knaves and fools combined o'er all prevail,
And weigh their Justice in a Golden Scale;
E'en then the boldest start from public sneers,
Afraid of Shame, unknown to other fears,
More darkly[3] sin, by Satire kept in awe,
And shrink from Ridicule, though not from Law.

Such is the force of Wit! But not belong
To me the arrows of satiric song;
The royal vices of our age demand
A keener weapon, and a mightier hand.
Still there are follies, e'en for me to chase,
And yield at least amusement in the race:
Laugh when I laugh, I seek no other fame,
The cry is up, and scribblers are my game:
Speed, Pegasus!—ye strains of great and small,
Ode! Epic! Elegy!—have at you all!

[1]nought–nothing
[2]harbinger–warning sign
[3]darkly–secretly

I, too, can scrawl, and once upon a time
I poured along the town a flood of rhyme,
A schoolboy freak, unworthy praise or blame;
I printed—older children do the same.
'Tis pleasant, sure, to see one's name in print;
A Book's a Book, altho' there's nothing in't.
Not that a Title's sounding charm can save
Or scrawl or scribbler from an equal grave…

\*\*\*

Time was, ere[4] yet in these degenerate days
Ignoble themes obtained mistaken praise,
When Sense and Wit with Poesy allied,
No fabled Graces, flourished side by side,
From the same fount their inspiration drew,
And, reared by Taste, bloomed fairer as they grew.
Then, in this happy Isle, a POPE'S pure strain
Sought the rapt soul to charm, nor sought in vain;
A polished nation's praise aspired to claim,
And raised the people's, as the poet's fame.
Like him great DRYDEN poured the tide of song,
In stream less smooth, indeed, yet doubly strong…

But why these names, or greater still, retrace,
When all to feebler Bards resign their place?
Yet to such times our lingering looks are cast,
When taste and reason with those times are past.
Now look around, and turn each trifling page,
Survey the precious works that please the age;
This truth at least let Satire's self allow,
No dearth of Bards can be complained of now.
The loaded Press[5] beneath her labour groans,
And Printers' devils shake their weary bones;
While SOUTHEY'S Epics cram the creaking shelves,
And LITTLE'S Lyrics shine in hot-pressed twelves.[6]

[4]ere–before
[5]Press–printing press
[6]twelves–books folded into twelve sheets

**Questions:**

1. What purpose does satire serve, according to Byron?

2. How does Byron judge his own skills as a satirist? What is his intention in writing this poem, according to the second stanza?

3. What kinds of writers are the target of Byron's satire? Why does he satirize them?

4. What does Byron say about how poetry used to be? What poets were responsible?

5. What is the problem with the poets of Byron's own time?

**Activity:**

From the point of view of a modern musical artist, write a brief satire criticizing other musicians. Mention them by name, as Byron does here.

In his long poem *Don Juan*, Byron takes on a popular Romantic subject: the story of the famous Spanish seducer Don Juan. The form that Byron writes in had also been used by Italian and English poets for grand works, called *epics*, dealing with legendary heroes or lovers. Because Byron twists this grand rhyme and rhythm to fit his own humorous purposes, his poem is called a *mock-epic*.

### from *Don Juan*

### Canto One

#### XVIII

Perfect she[1] was, but as perfection is
Insipid[2] in this naughty world of ours,
Where our first parents never learn'd to kiss
Till they were exiled from their earlier bowers,[3]
Where all was peace, and innocence, and bliss
(I wonder how they got through the twelve hours),
Don Jóse,[4] like a lineal son of Eve,
Went plucking various fruit without her leave.

#### XIX

He was a mortal of the careless kind,
With no great love for learning, or the learned,
Who chose to go where'er he had a mind,
And never dreamed his lady was concerned;
The world, as usual, wickedly inclined
To see a kingdom or a house o'erturned,
Whispered he had a mistress, some said two.
But for domestic quarrels one will do.
**\*\*\*\***

#### XXIII

Don Jose and his lady quarreled—why,
Not any of the many could divine,
Though several thousand people chose to try,
'Twas surely no concern of theirs nor mine;

[1]She–Donna Inez, Don Juan's mother
[2]insipid–boring
[3]bowers–cool, shady spots
[4]Don Jose–Don Juan's father

I loathe that low vice—curiosity;
But if there's anything in which I shine,
'Tis in arranging all my friends' affairs,
Not having, of my own, domestic cares.

\*\*\*\*

### XXVI

Don Jose and the Donna Inez led
For some time an unhappy sort of life,
Wishing each other, not divorced, but dead;
They lived respectably as man and wife,
Their conduct was exceedingly well-bred,
And gave no outward signs of inward strife,
Until at length the smothered fire broke out,
And put the business past all kind of doubt.

\*\*\*\*

### XXVIII

She kept a journal, where his faults were noted,
And opened certain trunks of books and letters,
All which might, if occasion served, be quoted;
And then she had all Seville for abettors,[5]
Besides her good old grandmother (who doted[6]);
The hearers of her case became repeaters,
Then advocates, inquisitors, and judges,
Some for amusement, others for old grudges.

### XXIX

And then this best and meekest woman bore
With such serenity her husband's woes,
Just as the Spartan[7] ladies did of yore,
Who saw their spouses killed, and nobly chose
Never to say a word about them more—
Calmly she heard each calumny[8] that rose,
And saw his agonies with such sublimity,
That all the world exclaimed, "What magnanimity!"

\*\*\*\*

[5]abettors—helpers
[6]doted—was senile
[7]Spartan—from Sparta, an early Greek city famous for
    brave, unemotional citizens
[8]calumny—insult

### XXXII

Their friends had tried at reconciliation,
Then their relations, who made matters worse.
('Twere hard to tell upon a like occasion
To whom it may be best to have recourse—
I can't say much for friend or yet relation):
The lawyers did their utmost for divorce,
But scarce a fee was paid on either side
Before, unluckily, Don Jose died.

**\*\*\*\***

### LV

Amongst her numerous acquaintance, all
Selected for discretion and devotion,
There was the Donna Julia, whom to call
Pretty were but to give a feeble notion
Of many charms in her as natural
As sweetness to the flower, or salt to Ocean,
Her zone to Venus, or his bow to Cupid
(But this last simile is trite and stupid.)

**\*\*\*\***

### LXII

Wedded she was some years, and to a man
Of fifty, and such husbands are in plenty;
And yet, I think, instead of such a one
'Twere better to have two of five-and-twenty,
Especially in countries near the sun:
And now I think on it, *"mi vien in mente,"*[9]
Ladies even of the most uneasy virtue
Prefer a spouse whose age is short of thirty.

### LXIII

'Tis a sad thing, I cannot choose but say,
And all the fault of that indecent sun,
Who cannot leave alone our helpless clay,
But will keep baking, broiling, burning on,
That howsoever people fast and pray,
The flesh is frail, and so the soul undone:
What men call gallantry and gods adultery,
Is much more common where the climate's sultry.

[9]"mi vien in mente"–it comes to mind

### LXIV

Happy the nations of the moral North!
Where all is virtue, and the winter season
Sends sin, without a rag on, shivering forth
('Twas snow that brought St. Anthony to reason);
Where juries cast up what a wife is worth,
By laying whate'er sum, in mulct,[10] they please on
The lover, who must pay a handsome price,
Because it is a marketable vice.

### LXV

Alfonso was the name of Julia's lord,
A man well looking for his years, and who
Was neither much beloved nor yet abhorred:
They lived together as most people do,
Suffering each other's foibles by accord,
And not exactly either one or two;
Yet he was jealous, though he did not show it,
For Jealousy dislikes the world to know it.

### LXVI

Julia was—yet I never could see why—
With Donna Inez quite a favorite friend;
Between their tastes there was small sympathy,
For not a line had Julia ever penned:
Some people whisper (but, no doubt, they lie,
For Malice still imputes some private end)
That Inez had, ere Don Alfonso's marriage,
Forgot with him her very prudent carriage;

### LXVII

And that still keeping up the old connection,
Which Time had lately rendered much more chaste,
She took his lady also in affection,
And certainly this course was much the best:
She flattered Julia with her sage protection,
And complimented Don Alfonso's taste;
And if she could not (who can?) silence scandal,
At least she left it a more slender handle.

[10]mulct–penalty

### LXVIII

I can't tell whether Julia saw the affair
With other people's eyes, or if her own
Discoveries made, but none could be aware
Of this, at least no symptom e'er was shown;
Perhaps she did not know, or did not care,
Indifferent from the first, or callous grown:
I'm really puzzled what to think or say,
She kept her counsel in so close a way.

### LXIX

Juan she saw, and, as a pretty child,
Caressed him often—such a thing might be
Quite innocently done, and harmless styled,
When she had twenty years, and thirteen he;
But I am not so sure I should have smiled
When he was sixteen, Julia twenty-three;
These few short years make wondrous alterations,
Particularly amongst sun-burnt nations.

\* \* \* \*

### LXXV

Poor Julia's heart was in an awkward state;
She felt it going, and resolved to make
The noblest efforts for herself and mate,
For Honour's, Pride's, Religion's, Virtue's sake:
Her resolutions were most truly great,
And almost might have made a Tarquin[11] quake:
She prayed the Virgin Mary for her grace,
As being the best judge of a lady's case.

### LXXVI

She vowed she never would see Juan more,
And next day paid a visit to his mother,
And looked extremely at the opening door,
Which, by the Virgin's grace, let in another;
Grateful she was, and yet a little sore—
Again it opens, it can be no other,
'Tis surely Juan now—No! I'm afraid
That night the Virgin was no further prayed.

---

[11]Tarquin–family of early Roman kings; one was especially famous
for a brutal rape

### LXXVII

She now determined that a virtuous woman
Should rather face and overcome temptation,
That flight was base and dastardly, and no man
Should ever give her heart the least sensation,
That is to say, a thought beyond the common
Preference, that we must feel, upon occasion,
For people who are pleasanter than others,
But then they only seem so many brothers.

### LXXVIII

And even if by chance—and who can tell?
The Devil's so very sly—she should discover
That all within was not so very well,
And, if still free, that such or such a lover
Might please perhaps, a virtuous wife can quell
Such thoughts, and be the better when they're over:
And if the man should ask, 'tis but denial:
I recommend young ladies to make trial.

### LXXIX

And, then, there are such things as Love divine,
Bright and immaculate, unmixed and pure,
Such as the angels think so very fine,
And matrons, who would be no less secure,
Platonic,[12] perfect, "just such love as mine;"
Thus Julia said—and thought so, to be sure;
And so I'd have her think, were I the man
On whom her reveries celestial ran.

[12]Platonic–ideal

**Questions:**

1. Byron says that Donna Inez was perfect. Why, then did Don Jose not remain faithful to her? Is this a fault particular to Don Jose, or is it universal to all human beings?

2. What is ironic about the line "they lived respectably as man and wife"?

3. What tone is Byron using when he calls Donna Inez "the best and meekest woman"? What did Donna Inez do when Don Jose way unfaithful?

4. Why is it "unlucky" that Don Jose died?

5. How does Byron excuse the above-average adultery rate in Spain?

6. How does the "virtuous" North treat adultery?

7. Why does Byron say that if he were the object of Julia's affection, he would encourage her ideas about divine love?

8. Does this satire have a particular target?

The next excerpt, from the Ninth Canto of *Don Juan*, contains a section dealing with the danger of bad government. Although Wellington did defeat his enemy, says Byron, Britain is now suffering under his poor leadership.

### *from* Canto The Ninth

#### I

Oh, Wellington![1] (or "Villainton" —For Fame
Sounds the heroic syllables both ways;
France could not even conquer your great name,
But punned it down to this facetious[2] phrase—
Beating or beaten she will laugh the same, )
You have obtained great pensions and much praise:
Glory like yours should any dare gainsay,[3]
Humanity would rise, and thunder "Nay!"

\*\*\*\*

#### III

Though Britain owes (and pays you too) so much,
Yet Europe doubtless owes you greatly more:
You have repaired Legitimacy's crutch,
A prop not quite so certain as before:
The Spanish, and the French, as well as Dutch,
Have seen, and felt, how strongly you restore;
And Waterloo has made the world your debtor
(I wish your bards would sing it rather better) .

#### IV

You are "the best of cut-throats:" do not start;[4]
The phrase is Shakespeare's, and not misapplied:—
War's a brain-spattering, windpipe-slitting art,
Unless her cause by right be sanctified.
If you have acted once a generous part,
The World, not the World's masters, will decide,
And I shall be delighted to learn who,
Save you and yours, have gained by Waterloo?

[1]Wellington–British duke who defeated the French general
    Napoleon at the Battle of Waterloo (1815), preventing France
    from dominating Europe
[2]facetious–not serious; mocking
[3]gainsay–deny
[4]start–be startled, be surprised

### V

I am no flatterer—you've supped full of flattery:
They say you like it too— 'tis no great wonder.
He whose whole life has been assault and battery,
At last may get a little tired of thunder;
And swallowing eulogy[5] much more than satire, he
May like being praised for every lucky blunder,
Called "Saviour of the Nations"—not yet saved,—
And "Europe's Liberator"—still enslaved.

### VI

I've done. Now go and dine from off the plate
Presented by the Prince of the Brazils,
And send the sentinel before your gate
A slice or two from your luxurious meals:
He fought, but has not fed so well of late.
Some hunger too, they say the people feels:—
There is no doubt that you deserve your ration,
But pray give back a little to the nation.
                         ****

### VIII

Great men have always scorned great recompenses:
Epaminondas[6] saved his Thebes, and died,
Not leaving even his funeral expenses:
George Washington had thanks, and nought beside,
Except the all cloudless glory (which few men's is)
To free his country: Pitt[7] too had his pride,
And as a high-souled Minister of state is
Renowned for ruining Great Britain gratis.[8]

---

[5]eulogy–praise
[6]Epaminondas–general who died defending the ancient
    city of Thebes
[7]Pitt–Prime Minister of Britain
[8]gratis–free of charge

### IX

Never had mortal man such opportunity,
Except Napoleon, or abused it more:
You might have freed fallen Europe from the unity
Of Tyrants, and been blest from shore to shore:
And now—what is your fame? Shall the Muse tune it ye?
Now—that the rabble's first vain shouts are o'er?
Go! hear it in your famished country's cries!
Behold the World! and curse your victories!

### X

As these new cantos touch on warlike feats,
To you the unflattering Muse deigns to inscribe
Truths, that you will not read in the Gazettes,
But which 'tis time to teach the hireling tribe
Who fatten on their country's gore, and debts,
Must be recited—and without a bribe.
You did great things, but not being great in mind,
Have left undone the greatest—and mankind.

           ****

### XX

Oh! ye immortal Gods! what is Theogony?[9]
Oh! thou, too, mortal man! what is Philanthropy?[10]
Oh! World, which was and is, what is Cosmogony?[11]
Some people have accused me of Misanthropy;[12]
And yet I know no more than the mahogany
That forms this desk, of what they mean;—*Lykanthropy*[13]
I comprehend, for without transformation
Men become wolves on any slight occasion.

           ****

[9]theogony–study of the origin of the gods
[10]philanthropy–practice of giving to others
[11]cosmogony–study of the origins of the universe
[12]misanthropy–hatred of mankind
[13]lykanthropy–process by which man changes into a wolf

XXV

It is not that I adulate the people:
Without me, there are demagogues[14] enough,
And infidels,[15] to pull down every steeple,
And set up in their stead some proper stuff.
Whether they may sow skepticism to reap Hell,
As is the Christian dogma[16] rather rough,[17]
I do not know;—I wish men to be free
As much from mobs as kings—from you as me.

[14]demagogues–rulers who lead people by persuasion
[15]infidels–non-Christians
[16]dogma–teaching
[17]rough–roughly; in brief

## Questions:

1. Where in stanza VI does Byron use understatement? What is he emphasizing?

2. Why, according to Byron, is Pitt "renowned"?

3. What does Byron say about men who try to rule in place of the Church?

4. What does Byron seem to think of Wellington? Is Wellington the target of this section?

# Modern Poetry

## Stephen Crane

Crane (1871-1900) was a journalist who wrote novels and short stories in addition to poems. The war he mentions is the Civil War, which is also at the center of his novel, *The Red Badge of Courage.*

### War is Kind

Do not weep, maiden, for war is kind.
Because your lover threw wild hands toward the sky
And the affrighted steed ran on alone,
Do not weep
War is kind.

Hoarse, booming drums of the regiment,
Little souls who thirst for fight,
These men were born to drill and die.
The unexplained glory flies above them,
Great is the battle-god, great, and his kingdom–
A field where a thousand corpses lie.

Do not weep, babe, for war is kind.
Because your father tumbled in the yellow trenches,
Raged at his breast, gulped and died,
Do not weep.
War is kind.

Swift blazing flag of the regiment,
Eagle with crest of red and gold,
These men were born to drill and die.
Point for them the virtue of slaughter,
Make plain to them the excellence of killing
And a field where a thousand corpses lie.

Mother whose heart hung humble as a button
On the bright splendid shroud of your son,
Do not weep.
War is kind.

## Questions:

1. Who is speaking in this poem? What is the speaker's tone?

2. In the first and third stanzas, Crane reverses normal syntax; instead of saying "Do not weep because something happened," he says, "Because something happened, do not weep." What is he emphasizing by using this sentence order?

3. What colors and sounds does the author bring up when he describes the battle scenes? How does he then undermine these details?

4. Why is the title of the poem ironic?

# Siegfried Sassoon

The English writer Siegfried Sassoon (1886-1967) was part of what is known as the "Lost Generation," the group of young men whose minds and bodies were destroyed by World War I. His poems vividly describe his experiences fighting on the War's Western Front.

In the poem below, "scarlet Majors" refers to rear-echelon staff officers, who were stationed safely behind the front lines. Since they did not have to worry about being shot by snipers, they could afford to look very sporty in their red hatbands and lapel tabs.

### Base Details

If I were fierce, and bald, and short of breath,
I'd live with scarlet Majors at the Base,
And speed glum heroes up the line to death.
You'd see me with my puffy petulant face,
Guzzling and gulping in the best hotel,
Reading the Roll of Honor. "Poor young chap,"
I'd say—"I used to know his father well;
Yes, we've lost heavily in this last scrap."
And when the war is done and youth stone dead,
I'd toddle safely home and die—in bed.


**Questions:**

1.  Who is the speaker?

2.  Is he an officer or a soldier? How can you tell?

3.  What is ironic about the use of the word "heroes" in the third line?

4.  What, according to the speaker, do the officers do while soldiers die in battle?

5.  Read the poem aloud. How might the speaker's voice sound when he imitates the officer?

6. Why is the title ironic?

7. How is this war poem different from the one you read by Stephen Crane?

# CHAPTER IV

## SATIRE IN FICTION

## Miguel de Cervantes

At the beginning of the 17th century, the Spanish writer Miguel de Cervantes published the first part of the novel *Don Quixote*. In it, Don Quixote, an ordinary, elderly Spanish gentleman, obsessed with the romantic stories he has read, has himself dubbed a knight and sets out on a quest to right wrongs and correct injustice. For much of the journey, he is accompanied by Sancho Panza, an ignorant peasant whom he calls his "squire."

*Don Quixote* is a PARODY of popular Spanish romances. For more information on parody, see page 9.

### Don Quixote

AT THAT MOMENT they [Don Quixote and Sancho Panza] caught sight of some thirty or forty windmills, which stand on that plain. As soon as Don Quixote saw them he said to his squire: "Fortune is guiding our affairs better than we could have wished. Look over there, friend Sancho Panza. There are more than thirty monstrous giants. I intend to do battle with them and kill them all. It is a great service to God to wipe such a wicked brood from the face of the earth."

"What giants?" asked Sancho Panza.

"Those there, with the long arms."

"Take care, your worship," said Sancho; "those things over there are not giants but windmills. What seem to be their arms are the sails, which are whirled round in the wind and make the millstone turn."

"It is quite clear," replied Don Quixote, "that you are not experienced in this matter of adventures. They are giants, and if you are afraid, go away and say your prayers, while I advance and engage them in fierce and unequal battle."

As he spoke, he dug his spurs into his horse Rocinante, paying no attention to his squire's shouted warning that beyond all doubt they were windmills and not giants he was advancing to attack. Don Quixote went forward shouting in a loud voice: "Do not flee, cowards, for it is one knight alone who assails you."

At that moment a slight wind arose, and the great sails began to move. At the sight of which Don Quixote shouted: "Though you wield more arms than the giant Briareus,[1] you shall pay for it!" Then covering himself with his shield and putting his lance in the rest position, Don Quixote urged Rocinante forward at a full gallop and attacked the nearest windmill, thrusting his lance into the sail. But the wind turned it with such violence that it caught his weapon, dragging the horse and his rider with it, and sent the knight rolling badly injured across the ground. Sancho Panza rushed to his assistance.

"Oh my goodness!" cried Sancho. "Didn't I tell your worship to look what you were doing, for they were only windmills? Nobody could mistake them, unless he had windmills on the brain."

"Silence, friend Sancho," replied Don Quixote. "Matters of war are more subject than most to continual change. What is more, I think that the same wizard who robbed me of my books has turned those giants into windmills, to cheat me of the glory of conquering them. Such is the hatred he bears me."

As they discussed this last adventure Don Quixote was much concerned at the loss of his lance, and, speaking of it to his squire, remarked: "I remember reading that a certain Spanish knight, having broken his sword in battle, tore a great limb from an oak and pounded so many Moors,[2] that he earned the surname of the Pounder. I mention this because I plan to tear down just such a limb and do such deeds with it that you may consider yourself most fortunate to have seen them."

They passed that night under some trees. From one of these trees Don Quixote tore down a dead branch to serve as his lance, and stuck into it the iron head of the one that had been broken. And all night Don Quixote did not sleep but thought about his Lady Dulcinea. This conformed to what he had read in his books about knight errants spending many sleepless nights dwelling on the memory of their ladies. Not so Sancho Panza; for, as his stomach was full, and not of water, he slept right through till morning. And, if his master had not called him, neither the sunbeams, which struck him full on the face, nor the song of the birds would have been enough to wake him. As he got up he held up his bottle, and found it emptier than the night before; his heart sank, for he did not think they were taking the right road to remedy this defect very quickly. Don Quixote wanted no breakfast for, as we have said, he was determined to subsist on memories. Then they turned back on to the road they had been on before.

"Here," exclaimed Don Quixote on seeing it, "here, brother Sancho Panza, we can steep our arms to the elbows in what they call adventures. But take note

---

[1]Briareus–mythological monster with one hundred hands and fifty heads
[2]Moors–Muslims who moved into Spain from Africa

that though you see me in the greatest danger in the world, you must not put your hand to your sword to defend me, unless you know that my assailants are rabble and common folk; in which case you may come to my aid. But should they be knights, on no account will it be legal or permissible, by the laws of chivalry, for you to assist me until you are yourself knighted."

"You may be sure, sir," replied Sancho, "that I shall obey your worship perfectly there. Especially as I am very peaceable by nature and all against shoving myself in to brawls and quarrels. But as to defending myself, sir, I shan't take much notice of those rules, because divine law and human law allow everyone to defend himself against anyone who tries to harm him."

"I never said otherwise," replied Don Quixote, "but in the matter of aiding me against knights, you must restrain your natural impulses."

"I promise you I will," replied Sancho, "and I will observe this rule as strictly as the Sabbath."

In the middle of this conversation two monks of the order of St. Benedict appeared on the road, mounted on what looked like camels; for the two mules they were riding were quite big. They were wearing riding masks against the dust and carrying sunshades. Behind them came a coach, with four or five horsemen escorting it.

In the coach, as it afterwards turned out, was a Basque lady traveling to Seville to join her husband. The monks were not of her company, but merely journeying on the same road.

Now no sooner did Don Quixote see them in the distance than he said to his squire, "Either I am much mistaken, or this will prove the most famous adventure ever seen. For those dark shapes looming over there must be, beyond all doubt, enchanters bearing off in that coach some princess they have stolen; and it is my duty to redress this wrong with all my might."

## Questions:

1. What ordinary things are transformed by Don Quixote's grand vision?

2. What detail does Cervantes include to remind the reader that Sancho Panza is just an ordinary peasant?

3. Who seems to be speaking in this passage? What is the speaker's tone?

4. What do you think Cervantes is making fun of?

# Jonathan Swift

## Gulliver's Travels

In Book I, Gulliver was shipwrecked on the island of Lilliput, a land inhabited by people sixty times smaller than he. Here, in the land of Brobdingnag, he is much smaller than the inhabitants.

## from Book II, Chapter Six

HE [the king of Brobdingnag] was perfectly astonished with the historical account I gave him of our affairs in England during the last century, protesting it was only a heap of conspiracies, rebellions, murders, massacres, revolutions, banishments, the very worst effects that avarice,[1] faction, hypocrisy, perfidiousness,[2] cruelty, rage, madness, hatred, envy, lust, malice, or ambition could produce.

...Then taking me into his hands, and stroking me gently, he spoke these words, which I shall never forget, nor the manner he spoke them in: "My little friend Grildrig; you have made a most admirable speech upon your country. You have clearly proved that ignorance, idleness and vice may be sometimes the only ingredients for qualifying a legislator. That laws are best explained, interpreted, and applied by those whose interest and abilities lie in perverting, confounding, and eluding them. I observe among you some lines of an institution, which in its original might have been tolerable, but since has become corrupted. It does not appear from all you have said, how any one virtue is required towards the just procurement of any one station[3] among you, much less that men were ennobled on account of their virtue, that priests were advanced for their piety or learning, soldiers for their conduct or valor, judges for their integrity, senators for the love of their country, or counselors for their wisdom. As for yourself," continued the King, "who have spent the greatest part of your life in traveling, I am well disposed to hope you may hitherto have escaped many vices of your country. But, by what I have gathered from your own talk I cannot but conclude the bulk of your natives, to be the most evil race of little odious vermin that Nature ever suffered to crawl upon the surface of the earth.

[1]avarice–greed
[2]perfidiousness–betrayal, disloyalty
[3]station–office

## Questions:

1. Why does Swift emphasize the king's amazement at Gulliver's story?

2. What does it take to become a lawmaker, according to the conclusion the king draws from Gulliver's story?

3. Why does the king think Gulliver may not be as bad as his countrymen?

4. Who is the target of the satire in this excerpt?

**from Book III, Chapter Two . . . .**

Gulliver finds himself in Laputa, a land ruled by a king on a flying island.

AT MY ALIGHTING I was surrounded by a crowd of people, but those who stood nearest seemed to be of better quality. They beheld me with all the marks and circumstances of wonder, neither indeed was I much in their debt; having never till then seen a race of mortals so singular in their shapes, habits, and countenances.[1] Their heads were all reclined either to the right, or the left; one of their eyes turned inward, and the other directly up to the zenith.[2] Their outer garments were adorned with the figures of suns, moons, and stars, interwoven with those of fiddles, flutes, harps, trumpets, guitars, harpsichords, and many more instruments of music, unknown to us in Europe. I observed here and there many dressed as servants, with a blown bladder fastened like a flail to the end of a short stick, which they carried in their hands. In each bladder was a small quantity of dried peas or little pebbles, (as I was afterwards informed). With these bladders they now and then flapped the mouths and ears of those who stood near them, of which practice I could not then understand the meaning; it seems, the minds of these people are so taken up with intense speculations, that they neither can speak, nor attend to the speech of others, without being roused by some external touch upon the organs of speech and hearing; for which reason, those persons who are able to afford it always keep a flapper, in their family, as one of their domestics,[3] nor ever walk abroad or make visits without him. And the business of this officer is, when two or three more persons are in company, gently to strike with his bladder the mouth of him who is to speak, and the right ear of him or them to whom the speaker addresses himself. This flapper is likewise employed to attend his master in his walks, and upon occasion to give him a soft flap on his eyes, because he is always so wrapped up in thought, that he is in manifest[4] danger of falling down every precipice,[5] and bouncing his head against every post, and in the streets, of jostling others or being jostled himself into the gutter.

It was necessary to give the reader this information, without which he would be at a loss, to understand the proceedings of these people, as they conducted me up the stairs, to the top of the island, and from thence to the royal palace. While we were ascending, they forgot several times what they were about, and left me to myself, till their memories were again roused by their flappers.

[1]countenances–facial expressions
[2]zenith–heavens; top of the sky
[3]domestics–servants
[4]precipice–hill
[5]manifest–clear

At last we entered the palace, and proceeded into the chamber of the King seated on his throne, attended on each side by persons of prime quality. Before the throne, was a large table filled with globes and spheres, and mathematical instruments of all kinds. His Majesty took not the least notice of us, although our entrance was not without sufficient noise, by the concourse of all persons belonging to the Court. But, he was then deep in a problem, and we attended at least an hour, before he could solve it. Standing by him on each side, were young pages, with flaps in their hands, and when they saw he was at leisure, one of them gently struck his mouth, and the other his right ear, at which he started like one awaked on the sudden, and looking towards me, and the company I was in, recollected the occasion of our coming, whereof he had been informed before. He spoke some words, whereupon immediately a young man with a flap came up to my side, and flapped me gently on the right ear, but I made signs as well as I could, that I had no occasion for such an instrument; which as I afterwards found gave his Majesty and the whole Court a very mean opinion of my understanding. The King, as far as I could conjecture, asked me several questions, and I addressed myself to him in all the languages I had. When it was found, that I could neither understand nor be understood, I was conducted by the King's order to an apartment in his palace, where two servants were appointed to attend me. My dinner was brought, and four persons of quality, whom I remembered to have seen very near the King's person, did me the honor to dine with me. We had two courses, of three dishes each. In the first course, there was a shoulder of mutton, cut into an equilateral triangle, a piece of beef into a rhomboid, and a pudding into a cycloid. The second course was two ducks, trussed[6] up into the form of fiddles; sausages and puddings resembling flutes and violins, and a breast of veal in the shape of a harp. The servants cut our bread into cones, cylinders, parallelograms, and several other mathematical figures.

Those to whom the King had entrusted me, observing how ill I was dressed ordered a tailor to come next morning, and take my measure for a suit of clothes. This operator did his office after a different manner from those of his trade in Europe. He first took my altitude by a quadrant,[7] and then with rule and compasses, described the dimensions and outlines of my whole body, all which he entered upon paper, and in six days brought my clothes very ill made, and quite out of shape, by happening to mistake a figure in the calculation. But my comfort was, that I observed such accidents happened very frequently and were little regarded.

. . . . .

[6]trussed—with wings bound
[7]quadrant—instrument for measuring angles

The knowledge I had in mathematics gave me great assistance in acquiring their phraseology, which depended much upon that science and music; and in the latter I was not unskilled. Their ideas are perpetually conversant[8] in lines and figures. If they would, for example, praise the beauty of a woman or any other animal, they describe it by rhombus, circles, parallelograms, ellipses, and other geometrical terms, or by words of art drawn from music, needless here to repeat. I observed in the King's kitchen all sorts of mathematical and musical instruments, after the figures of which they cut up the joints that were served to his Majesty's table.

Their houses are very ill built, the walls bevel,[9] without one right angle in any apartment, and this defect arises from the contempt they have for practical geometry; which they despise as vulgar and mechanic, those instructions they give being too refined for the minds of their workmen, which causes perpetual mistakes. And although these people are dexterous[10] enough upon a piece of paper in the management of the rule, the pencil and the divider, yet in the common actions and behavior of life, I have not seen a more clumsy, awkward, and unhandy people, nor so slow and perplexed in their conceptions upon all other subjects, except those of mathematics and music. They are very bad reasoners, and vehemently given to opposition, unless when they happen to be of the right opinion, which is seldom their case. Of imagination, fancy, and invention, they are wholly strangers, nor have they any words in their language by which those ideas can be expressed; the whole compass of their thoughts and mind being shut up within the two aforementioned sciences.

Most of them, and especially those who deal in the astronomical part, have great faith in astrology, although they are ashamed to own it publicly. But, what I thought altogether unaccountable, was the strong disposition I observed in them towards news and politics, perpetually inquiring into public affairs, giving their judgments in matters of state; and passionately disputing every inch of a party opinion. I have indeed observed the same disposition among most of the mathematicians I have known in Europe, although I could never discover the least analogy between the two sciences; unless those people suppose, that because the smallest circle has as many degrees as the largest, therefore the regulation and management of the world require no more abilities than the handling and turning of a globe. But, I rather take this quality to spring from a very common infirmity of human nature, inclining us to be more curious and conceited in matters where we have least concern, and for which we are least adapted either by study or nature.

These people are never able to enjoy a minute's peace of mind; and their disturbances proceed from causes which very little affect the rest of mortals. Their

[8]conversant–able to speak
[9]bevel–sloping
[10]dexterous–skillful

fears arise from several changes they dread in the celestial bodies. For instance, that the earth by the continual approaches of the sun towards it, must in course of time be absorbed or swallowed up. That the face of the sun will by degrees be encrusted with its own gases, and give no more light to the world. That, the earth very narrowly escaped a brush from the tail of the last comet, which would have infallibly reduced it to ashes; and that the next, which they have calculated for one and thirty years hence, will probably destroy us. For, if in its path it should approach within a certain degree of the sun, (as by their calculations they have reason to dread) it will experience a degree of heat ten thousand times more intense than that of red-hot glowing iron; and in its passage away from the sun, carry a blazing tail ten hundred thousand and fourteen miles long; through which if the earth should pass at the distance of one hundred thousand miles from the nucleus of the comet, the earth must in its passage be set on fire, and reduced to ashes. That the sun daily spending its rays without any nutriment to supply them, will at last be wholly consumed and annihilated; which must be attended with the destruction of this earth, and of all the planets that receive their light from it.

These people are so perpetually alarmed with the apprehensions of these and the like impending dangers, that they can neither sleep quietly in their beds, nor have any relish for the common pleasures or amusements of life. When they meet an acquaintance in the morning, the first question is about the sun's health, how he looked at his setting and rising, and what hopes they have to avoid the stroke of the approaching comet. This conversation they are apt to run into with the same temper that boys discover, in delighting to hear terrible stories of spirits and hobgoblins, which they greedily listen to, and dare not go to bed for fear.

The women of the island have an abundance of high spirits; they condemn their husbands, and are exceedingly fond of strangers. Among these visiting strangers the ladies choose their lovers; but the vexation[11] is, that they act with too much ease and security, for the husband is always so rapt in speculation, that the mistress and lover may proceed to the greatest familiarities before his face, if he be but provided with paper and implements, and without his flapper at his side.

The wives and daughters lament their confinement to the island, but they are not allowed to leave without a particular license from the King; and this is not easy to be obtained, because the people of quality have found by frequent experience, how hard it is to persuade their women to return from below. I was told that a great Court lady, who has several children, is married to the Prime Minister, who is the richest subject in the kingdom, and is extremely fond of her, and lives in the finest palace of the island; she went down to Lagado, on the pretense of health, there hid herself for several months, till the King sent a warrant to search for her, and she was found in an obscure eating house all in rags, having pawned

[11]vexation—trouble

her clothes to maintain an old deformed footman, who beat her every day, and from whose company she was taken much against her will. And although her husband received her with all possible kindness, and without the least reproach, she soon after contrived to steal down again with all her jewels, to the same lover, and hath not been heard of since.

## Questions:

1.  Where do the Laputians live? Why is this significant?

2.  Describe the heads, eyes, and clothing of the Laputians. How do these characteristics illustrate the qualities Swift is satirizing?

3.  Why do the Laputians need servants?

4.  What is unusual about Gulliver's dinner?

5.  Why does Gulliver's suit not fit him?

6.  What kind of language do the Laputians speak?

7.  Why are the Laputian houses badly built?

8.  Why does Gulliver think the Laputians try to become involved in politics? What is Gulliver's opinion about the relationship betwen science and politics?

9.  What do the Laputians constantly worry about? What feature in their personalities leads them to this worry?

10. How do the Laputian women respond to the behavior of the men?

11. What kind of people are targeted in this satire?

## Research Opportunity:

Make a list of some of the kinds of people you think Swift may be mocking in this satire. Then, follow up your guess by researching Swift's time period. What famous people seem to fit the description Swift uses here? Did any of them read *Gulliver's Travels* or respond to it?

In Book IV, Gulliver meets two kinds of creatures. The first creatures, who look like humans, are called Yahoos; the second, horse-like beasts, are called Houyhnhnms.

### from Book IV, Chapter One

IN THIS DESOLATE condition I advanced forward, and soon got upon firm ground, where I sat down on a bank to rest myself, and consider what I had best to do. When I was a little refreshed, I went up into the country, resolving to deliver myself to the first savages I should meet, and purchase my life from them by some bracelets, glass rings, and other toys, which sailors usually provide themselves with in those voyages, and whereof I had some about me: the land was divided by long rows of trees not regularly planted, but naturally growing; there was great plenty of grass, and several fields of oats. I walked very circumspectly for fear of being surprised, or suddenly shot with an arrow from behind or on either side. I fell into a beaten road, where I saw many tracks of human feet, and some of cows, but most of horses. At last I beheld several animals in a field, and one or two of the same kind sitting in trees. Their shape was very singular, and deformed, which a little discomposed me, so that I lay down behind a thicket to observe them better. Some of them coming forward near the place where I lay, gave me an opportunity of distinctly marking their form. Their heads and breasts were covered with a thick hair, some frizzled and others lank, they had beards like goats, and a long ridge of hair down their backs, and the fore-parts of their legs and feet, but the rest of their bodies were bare, so that I might see their skins, which were of a brown buff color. They had no tails, nor any hair at all on their buttocks. They climbed high trees, as nimbly as a squirrel, for they had strong extended claws before and behind, terminating in sharp points, hooked. They would often spring, and bound, and leap with prodigious agility. The females were not so large as the males; they had long lank hair on their heads, and only a sort of down on the rest of their bodies, except about their privates. Their dugs hung between their forefeet, and often reached almost to the ground as they walked. The hair of both sexes was of several colors, brown, red, black and yellow. Upon the whole, I never beheld in all my travels so disagreeable an animal, nor one against which I naturally conceived so strong an antipathy. So that thinking I had seen enough, full of contempt and aversion, I got up and pursued the beaten road, hoping it might direct me to the cabin of some Indian. I had not gone far when I met one of these creatures full in my way, and coming up directly to me. The ugly monster, when he saw me, distorted several ways every feature of his visage, and stared as at an object he had never seen before; then approaching nearer, lifted up his forepaw, whether out of curiosity or mischief, I could not tell. But I drew my hanger,[1] and gave him a good blow with the flat side of it, for I durst not strike him with the edge, fearing the inhabitants might be provoked against me, if they should come to know, that I had killed or maimed any of their cattle. When the beast felt the smart, he drew back, and roared so loud, that a herd of at least forty came flocking about me from the next field, howling and making odious faces; but I ran to the body of a tree, and leaning my back against it, kept them off, by waving my hanger. Several of this cursed brood getting hold of the branches behind leapt up in the tree, from whence they began to discharge their excrements on my head: however, I escaped pretty well, by sticking close to the stem of the tree, but was almost stifled with the filth, which fell about me on every side.

In the midst of this distress, I observed them all to run away on a sudden as fast as they could, at which I ventured to leave the tree, and pursue the road, wondering what it was that could put them into this fright. But looking on my left hand, I saw a horse walking softly in the field: which my persecutors having sooner discovered, was the cause of their flight. The horse started a little when he came near me, but soon recovering himself, looked full in my face with manifest tokens of wonder: he viewed my hands and feet, walking round me several times. I would have pursued my journey, but he placed himself directly in the way, yet looking with a very mild aspect, never offering the least violence. We stood gazing at each other for some time; at last I took the boldness, to reach my hand towards his neck, with a design to stroke it, using the common style and whistle of jockeys when they are going to handle a strange horse. But this animal seeming to receive my civilities with disdain shook his head, and bent his brows, softly raising up his right forefoot to remove my hand. Then he neighed three or four times, but in so different a cadence, that I almost began to think he was speaking to himself in some language of his own.

While he and I were thus employed, another horse came up; who applying himself to the first in a very formal manner, they gently struck each other's right hoof before, neighing several times by turns, and varying the sound, which seemed to be almost articulate. They went some paces off, as if it were to confer together, walking side by side, backward and forward, like persons deliberating upon some affair of weight, but often turning their eyes towards me, as it were to watch that I might not escape. I was amazed to see such actions and behavior in brute beasts, and concluded with myself, that if the inhabitants of this country were endowed with a proportional degree of reason, they must needs be the wisest people upon

[1]hanger—short sword

earth. This thought gave me so much comfort, that I resolved to go forward until I could discover some house or village, or meet with any of the natives, leaving the two horses to discourse together as they pleased. But the first, who was a dapple-gray, observing me to steal off, neighed after me in so expressive a tone, that I fancied myself to understand what he meant; whereupon I turned back, and came near him, to expect his farther commands; but concealing my fear as much as I could, for I began to be in some pain, how this adventure might terminate; and the reader will easily believe I did not much like my present situation.

The two horses came up close to me, looking with great earnestness upon my face and hands. The gray steed rubbed my hat all round with his right forehoof, and discomposed it so much, that I was forced to adjust it better, by taking it off, and settling it again; whereat both he and his companion (who was a brown bay) appeared to be much surprised; the latter felt the lappet of my coat, and finding it to hang loose about me, they both looked with new signs of wonder. He stroked my right hand, seeming to admire the softness, and color; but he squeezed it so hard between his hoof and his pastern,[2] that I was forced to roar; after which they both touched me with all possible tenderness. They were under great perplexity about my shoes and stockings, which they felt very often, neighing to each other, and using various gestures, not unlike those of a philosopher, when he would attempt to solve some new and difficult phenomenon.

Upon the whole, the behavior of these animals was so orderly and rational, so acute and judicious,[3] that I at last concluded, they must needs be magicians, who had thus metamorphosed[4] themselves upon some design, and seeing a stranger in the way, were resolved to divert themselves with him; or perhaps were really amazed at the sight of a man so very different in habit, feature and complexion from those who might probably live in so remote a climate. Upon the strength of this reasoning, I ventured to address them in the following manner: Gentlemen, if you be conjurers, as I have good cause to believe, you can understand any language; therefore I make bold to let your worships know, that I am a poor distressed English man, driven by his misfortunes upon your coast, and I entreat one of you, to let me ride upon his back, as if he were a real horse, to some house or village, where I can be relieved. In return of which favor, I will make you a present of this knife and bracelet, (taking them out of my pocket.) The two creatures stood silent while I spoke, seeming to listen with great attention; and when I had ended, they neighed frequently towards each other, as if they were engaged in serious conversation. I plainly observed, that their language expressed

[2]pastern—part of a horse's foot behind the hoof
[3]judicious—well-thought-out
[4]metamorphosed—transformed

the passions very well, and the words might with little pains be resolved into an alphabet more easily than the Chinese.

I could frequently distinguish the word *Yahoo*, which was repeated by each of them several times; and although it was impossible for me to conjecture what it meant, yet while the two horses were busy in conversation, I endeavored to practice this word upon my tongue; and as soon as they were silent, I boldly pronounced Yahoo in a loud voice, imitating, at the same time, as near as I could, the neighing of a horse; at which they were both visibly surprised, and the gray repeated the same word twice, as if he meant to teach me the right accent, wherein I spoke after him as well as I could, and found myself perceivably to improve every time, though very far from any degree of perfection. Then the bay tried me with a second word, much harder to be pronounced; but reducing it to the English orthography, may be spelt thus, *Houyhnhnm*. I did not succeed in this so well as the former, but after two or three farther trials, I had better fortune; and they both appeared amazed at my capacity.

## Questions:

1. How do the Yahoos communicate? How do the Houyhnhnm communicate?

2. What differences in attitude do we see between the two groups?

3. What is Swift trying to tell us by emphasizing the contrast between the human-looking Yahoos and the horse-like Houyhnyms?

4. Who might be the target of this section?

**Essay Question:**

Read the following paragraph, which comes from a letter written by Gulliver to his nephew.

> Pray bring to your mind how often I desired you to consider, when you insisted on the motive of public good, that the Yahoos were a species of animals utterly incapable of amendment by precept or example: and so it has proved; for, instead of seeing a full stop put to all abuses and corruptions, at least in this little island, as I had reason to expect; behold, after above six months warning, I cannot learn that my book has produced one single effect according to my intentions.

Write about a similar experience in your own life. Who were the Yahoos in your story? How did you try to change them? Why did your efforts fail?

# Voltaire (Francois-Marie Arouet)

Voltaire (1694-1778) was a philosopher and freethinker who attacked both the Catholic Church and the government of France. In his novel *Candide*, Voltaire mocks the philosophy of the German Gottfried Liebniz, who claimed that our world, because it was created by a perfect God, must be the best of all possible worlds.

## Candide

### Chapter I

*How Candide was brought up in a Magnificent Castle, and how he was expelled from there.*

IN A CASTLE of Westphalia,[1] belonging to the Baron of Thunder-ten-Tronckh,[2] lived a youth, whom nature had endowed with the most gentle manners. His face was a true picture of his soul. He combined a true judgment with simplicity of spirit, which was the reason, I apprehend, of his being called Candide.[3] The old servants of the family suspected him to have been the son of the Baron's sister, by a good, honest gentleman of the neighborhood, whom that young lady would never marry because he had been able to prove only seventy-one quarterings,[4] the rest of his genealogical tree having been lost through the injuries of time.

The Baron was one of the most powerful lords in Westphalia, for his castle had not only a gate, but windows. His great hall, even, was hung with tapestry. All the dogs of his farmyards formed a pack of hounds when needed for a hunt; his grooms were his huntsmen; and the curate of the village was his grand almoner.[5] They called him "My Lord," and laughed at all his stories.

The Baron's lady weighed about three hundred and fifty pounds, and was therefore a person of great consideration, and she did the honours of the house with a dignity that commanded still greater respect. Her daughter Cunegonde was seventeen years of age, fresh-coloured, comely, plump, and desirable. The Baron's son seemed to be in every respect worthy of his father. Their tutor, Pangloss,[6] was the oracle of the family, and little Candide heard his lessons with all the good

[1]Westphalia–an area in Germany where the treaty that ended the Thirty Years' War was signed.

[2]Thunder-ten-Tronckh–with this name, Voltaire is mocking the gutteral German language

[3]Candide–His name means "honest," "candid," or "naive."

[4]quarterings–divisions on a coat of arms, showing the nobility of a  person's  family.

[5]almoner–person who distributes charity

[6]Pangloss–His name means "all tongues," and is a reference to the many languages he speaks

faith of his age and character.

Pangloss was professor of metaphy-sico-theologico-cosmolo-nigology. He proved admirably that there is no effect without a cause, and that, in this best of all possible worlds, the Baron's castle was the most magnificent of castles, and his lady the best of all possible Baronesses.

"It is demonstrable," said he, "that things cannot be otherwise than as they are; for all being created for an end, all is necessarily for the best end." He continued, "Observe, that the nose has been formed to bear spectacles—thus we have spectacles. Legs are visibly designed for stockings—and we have stockings. Stones were made to be hewn,[7] and to construct castles—therefore my lord has a magnificent castle; for the greatest baron in the province ought to be the best lodged. Pigs were made to be eaten—therefore we eat pork all the year round. Consequently they who assert that all is well have said a foolish thing, they should have said all is for the best."

Candide listened attentively and believed innocently; for he thought Miss Cunegonde extremely beautiful, though he never had the courage to tell her so. He concluded that after the happiness of being born Baron of Thunder-ten-Tronckh, the second degree of happiness was to be Miss Cunegonde, the third that of seeing her every day, and the fourth that of hearing Master Pangloss, the greatest philosopher of the whole province, and consequently of the whole world.

One day Cunegonde, while walking near the castle, in a little wood which they called a park, saw between the bushes, Dr. Pangloss giving a lesson in experimental natural philosophy to her mother's chambermaid, a little brown wench, very pretty and very docile. As Miss Cunegonde had a great disposition for the sciences, she breathlessly observed the repeated experiments of which she was a witness; she clearly perceived the force of the Doctor's reasons, the effects, and the causes; she turned back greatly flurried,[8] quite pensive,[9] and filled with the desire to be learned, dreaming that she might well be a sufficient reason for young Candide, and he for her.

She met Candide on reaching the castle and blushed; Candide blushed also; she wished him good morrow in a faltering tone, and Candide spoke to her without knowing what he said. The next day after dinner, as they went from the table, Cunegonde and Candide found themselves behind a screen; Cunegonde let fall her handkerchief; after Candide picked it up, she took him innocently by the hand, the youth as innocently kissed the young lady's hand with particular vivacity, sensibility, and grace; their lips met, their eyes sparkled, their knees trembled, their hands strayed. Baron Thunder-ten-tronckh passed near the screen

[7]hewn—cut
[8]flurried—excited
[9]pensive—preoccupied, full of thought

and beholding this cause and effect chased Candide from the castle with great kicks on the backside; Cunegonde fainted away; she was boxed on the ears by the Baroness, as soon as she came to herself; and all was consternation[10] in this most magnificent and most agreeable of all possible castles.

[10]consternation–turmoil, upset

## Questions:

1.  Why did the Baron's sister refuse to marry Candide's father?

2.  How can an observer tell, according to Voltaire, that the Baron is "one of the most powerful lords in Westphalia"?

3.  Why is the Baron's lady "of great consideration"? (Keep in mind that "great" and "large" are synonyms.)

4.  Describe the logic of Pangloss. What is wrong with it? Think of an example of this philosophy from your own environment.

5.  Based on Pangloss' theories about the world, Candide organizes his own life into "degrees of happiness." What is ridiculous about this system?

6.  What does Cunegonde see behind the bushes in the park? What language does Voltaire use to describe it? What is the effect of such language?

## Essay/Discussion Question:

Compare Pangloss to the Laputians of *Gulliver's Travels* (page 62).

# Chapter II

## *What became of Candide among the Bulgarians*

CANDIDE, DRIVEN FROM this earthly paradise, walked a long while without knowing where, weeping, raising his eyes to heaven, turning them often towards the most magnificent of castles which imprisoned the purest of noble young ladies. He lay down to sleep without supper, in the middle of a field between two furrows. The snow fell in large flakes. Next day Candide dragged himself towards the neighbouring town, which was called Waldberghofftrarbk-dikdorff; having no money, and dying of hunger and fatigue, Candide stopped sorrowfully at the door of an inn. Two men dressed in blue, soldier uniforms observed him.

"Comrade," said one, "here is a well-built young fellow, and of proper height."

They went up to Candide and very civilly invited him to dinner.

"Gentlemen," replied Candide, with a most engaging modesty, "you do me great honour, but I have not the wherewithal to pay my share."

"Oh, sir," said one of the blue uniforms to him, "people of your appearance and of your merit never pay anything: are you not five feet five inches high?"

"Yes, sir, that is my height," answered he, making a low bow.

"Come, sir, seat yourself; not only will we pay your reckoning, but we will never suffer such a man as you to want money; men are only born to assist one another."

"You are right," said Candide; "this is what I was always taught by Mr. Pangloss, and I see plainly that all is for the best."

They begged of him to accept a few crowns. He took them, and wished to give them his note; they refused; they seated themselves at table.

"Love you not deeply?"

"Oh, yes," answered he; "I deeply love Miss Cunegonde."

"No," said one of the gentlemen, "we ask you if you do not deeply love the King of the Bulgarians?"

"Not at all," said he; "for I have never seen him."

"What! he is the best of kings, and we must drink his health."

"Oh! very willingly, gentlemen," and he drank.

"That is enough," they tell him. "Now you are the help, the support, the defender, the hero of the Bulgarians. Your fortune is made, and your glory is assured."

Instantly they shackled him, and carried him away to the regiment. There he was made to march to the right, and to the left, to draw his rammer, to return his rammer, to present arms, to fire, to march again, and they gave him thirty blows with a cudgel. The next day he did his exercise a little less badly, and he received but twenty blows. The day following they gave him only ten, and he was regarded by his comrades as a fast learner.

Candide, all stupefied, could not yet very well realize how he was a hero. He resolved one fine day in spring to go for a walk, marching straight before him, believing that it was a privilege of the human as well as of the animal species to make use of their legs as they pleased. He had advanced two leagues[1] when he was overtaken by four others, heroes of six feet, who bound him and carried him to a dungeon. He was asked which he would like the best, to be whipped six-and-thirty times through all the regiment, or to receive at once twelve balls of lead in his brain. He vainly said that human will is free, and that he chose neither the one nor the other. He was forced to make a choice; he determined, in virtue of that gift of God called liberty, to run the gauntlet six-and-thirty times. He bore this twice. The regiment was composed of two thousand men; that composed for him four thousand strokes, which laid bare all his muscles and nerves, from the nape of his neck quite down to his rump. As they were going to proceed to a third whipping, Candide, able to bear no more, begged as a favour that they would be so good as to shoot him. He obtained this favour; they bandaged his eyes, and bade him kneel down. The King of the Bulgarians passed at this moment and learned the nature of the crime. As he had great talent, he understood from all that he learnt of Candide that he was a young metaphysician, extremely ignorant of the things of this world, and he accorded him his pardon with a clemency which will bring him praise in all the journals, and throughout all ages.

An able surgeon cured Candide in three weeks by means of emollients taught by Dioscorides. He had already a little skin, and was able to march when the King of the Bulgarians gave battle to the King of the Abares.

[1]league–about three miles

**Question:**

1.  How does Candide become the hero of the Bulgarians?

2.  What is Voltaire satirizing here?

## Chapter III

*How Candide made his escape from the Bulgarians, and what afterward became of him.*

THERE WAS NEVER anything so gallant, so spruce, so brilliant, and so well disposed as the two armies. Trumpets, fifes, drums, and cannons made music such as Hell itself had never heard. The cannons first of all laid flat about six thousand men on each side, the muskets swept away from this best of worlds nine or ten thousand ruffians who infested its surface. The bayonet was also a sufficient reason for the death of several thousands. The whole might have amounted to thirty thousand souls. Candide, who trembled like a philosopher, hid himself as well as he could during this heroic butchery.

At length, while the two kings were causing *Glory To God* to be sung each in his own camp, Candide resolved to go and reason elsewhere on effects and causes. He passed over heaps of dead and dying, and first reached a neighbouring village; it was in cinders, it was an Abare village which the Bulgarians had burnt according to the laws of war. Here, old men covered with wounds, beheld their wives, hugging their children to their bloody breasts, massacred before their faces; there, their daughters, disemboweled and breathing their last after having satisfied the natural wants of Bulgarian heroes; while others, half burnt in the flames, begged to be shot. The earth was strewed with brains, arms, and legs.

Candide fled quickly to another village; it belonged to the Bulgarians; and the Abarian heroes had treated it in the same way. Candide, walking always over trembling limbs or across ruins, arrived at last beyond the seat of war, with a few provisions in his knapsack, and Miss Cunegonde always in his heart. His provisions failed him when he arrived in Holland; but having heard that everybody was rich in that country, and that they were Christians, he did not doubt but he should meet with the same treatment from them as he had met with in the Baron's castle, before Miss Cunegonde's bright eyes were the cause of his expulsion thence. He asked alms of several grave-looking people, who all answered him, that if he continued to follow this trade they would confine him to the house of correction, where he should be taught to earn a living.

The next he addressed was a man who had been haranguing[1] a large assembly for a whole hour on the subject of charity. But the orator, looking askew, said:

"What are you doing here? Are you for the good cause?"

"There can be no effect without a cause," modestly answered Candide; "the whole is necessarily arranged for the best. It was necessary for me to have been banished from the presence of Miss Cunegonde, to have afterwards run the

---

[1]haranguing–harassing; ranting at

gauntlet, and now it is necessary I should beg my bread until I learn to earn it; all this cannot be otherwise."

"My friend," said the orator to him, "do you believe the Pope to be Anti-Christ?"

"I have not heard it," answered Candide; "but whether he be, or whether he be not, I want bread."

"Thou dost not deserve to eat," said the other. "Begone, rogue; begone, wretch; do not come near me again."

The orator's wife, putting her head out of the window, and spying a man that doubted whether the Pope was Anti-Christ, poured over him a full . . . Oh, heavens! to what excess does religious zeal carry the ladies.

A man who had never been christened, a good Anabaptist, named James, beheld the cruel treatment shown to one of his brethren, an unfeathered biped with a rational soul. Taking Candide home, James cleaned him, gave him bread and beer, presented him with two dollars, and even wished to teach him the manufacture of Persian stuffs which they make in Holland. Candide, almost prostrating himself before him, cried:

"Master Pangloss has well said that all is for the best in this world, for I am infinitely more touched by your extreme generosity than with the inhumanity of that gentleman in the black coat and his lady."

The next day on a walk he met a beggar all covered with scabs. The beggar's eyes were diseased, the end of his nose eaten away, his mouth distorted, his teeth black, choking in his throat, tormented with a violent cough, and spitting out a tooth at each effort.

[2]Anabaptist–a member of a religious group that believed adults, not infants, should receive baptism; noted for charity towards the poor

## Questions:

1. The narrator claims that the war was beneficial because it "swept away from this best of worlds nine or ten thousand ruffians who infested its surface." What is absurd about this statement?

2. Both armies sing *Glory to God*. Why is this detail noted? What point is the author making?

3. What important detail are we given about the only man who shows Candide any kindness? Why does Voltaire give this information?

## Chapter IV

*How Candide found his old master Pangloss, and what happened to them.*

CANDIDE, YET MORE moved with compassion than with horror, gave to this shocking beggar the two dollars which he had received from the honest Anabaptist James. The beggar looked at him very earnestly, dropped a few tears, and fell upon his neck. Candide recoiled in disgust.

"Alas!" said one wretch to the other, "do you no longer know your dear Pangloss?"

"What do I hear? You, my dear master! you in this terrible plight! What misfortune has happened to you? Why are you no longer in the most magnificent of castles? What has become of Miss Cunegonde, the pearl of girls, and nature's masterpiece?"

"I am so weak that I cannot stand," said Pangloss.

Upon which Candide carried him to the Anabaptist's stable, and gave him a crust of bread. As soon as Pangloss had refreshed himself a little:

"Well," said Candide, "How is Cunegonde?"

"She is dead," replied the other.

Candide fainted at this word; his friend recalled his senses with a little vinegar which he found by chance in the stable. Candide reopened his eyes.

"Cunegonde is dead! Ah, best of worlds, where art thou? But of what illness did she die? Was it not for grief, upon seeing her father kick me out of his magnificent castle?"

"No," said Pangloss, "she was ripped open by the Bulgarian soldiers, after having been violated by many; they broke the Baron's head for attempting to defend her; my lady, her mother, was cut in pieces; my poor pupil was served just in the same manner as his sister—and as for the castle, they have not left one stone upon another, not a barn, nor a sheep, nor a duck, nor a tree; but we have had our revenge, for the Abares have done the very same thing to a neighbouring barony, which belonged to a Bulgarian lord."

At this information Candide fainted again; but coming to himself, and having said all that it became him to say inquired into the cause and effect, as well as into the sufficient reason that had reduced Pangloss to so miserable a plight.

"Alas!" said the other, "it was love; love, the comfort of the human species, the preserver of the universe, the soul of all sensible beings, love, tender love."

"Alas!" said Candide, "I know this love, that sovereign of hearts, that soul of our souls; yet it never cost me more than a kiss and twenty kicks on the backside. How could this beautiful cause produce in you an effect so hateful?"

Pangloss made answer in these terms: "Oh, my dear Candide, you remember Paquette, that pretty wench who waited on our noble Baroness. In her arms I tasted the delights of paradise, which produced in me those hell torments with which you see me devoured; she was infected with them, she is perhaps dead of them. This present Paquette received of a learned Grey Friar, who had traced it to its source; he had had it of an old countess, who had received it from a cavalry captain, who owed it to a marchioness, who took it from a page, who had received it from a Jesuit, who when a novice had it in a direct line from one of the companions of Christopher Columbus. For my part, I shall give it to nobody, I am dying."

"Oh, Pangloss!" cried Candide, "what a strange genealogy! Is not the Devil the original stock of it?"

"Not at all," replied this great man, "it was a thing unavoidable, a necessary ingredient in the best of worlds; for if Columbus had not in an island of America caught this disease, which contaminates the source of life, frequently even hinders generation, and which is evidently opposed to the great end of nature, we should have neither chocolate nor cochineal.[1] We are also to observe that upon our continent, this distemper is like religious controversy, confined to a particular spot. The Turks, the Indians, the Persians, the Chinese, the Siamese, the Japanese, know nothing of it; but there is a sufficient reason for believing that they will know it in their turn in a few centuries. In the meantime, it has made marvellous progress among us, especially in those great armies composed of honest well-disciplined hirelings, who decide the destiny of states; for we may safely affirm that when an army of thirty thousand men fights another of an equal number, there are about twenty thousand of them p—x—d[2] on each side."

"Well, this is wonderful!" said Candide, "but you must get cured."

"Alas! how can I?" said Pangloss, "I have not a farthing, my friend, and all over the globe there is no letting of blood or taking a pee, without paying, or somebody paying for you."

These last words determined Candide; he went and flung himself at the feet of the charitable Anabaptist James, and gave him so touching a picture of the state to which his friend was reduced, that the good man did not hesitate to take Dr. Pangloss into his house, and had him cured at his expense. In the cure Pangloss lost only an eye and an ear. He wrote well, and knew arithmetic perfectly. The Anabaptist James made him his bookkeeper. At the end of two months, being obliged to go to Lisbon on some mercantile affairs, he took the two philosophers with him in his ship. Pangloss explained to him how everything was so constituted that it could not be better. James was not of this opinion.

"It is more likely," said he, "mankind has corrupted nature, for men were not born wolves, and they have become wolves; God has given them neither cannon of four-and-twenty pounders, nor bayonets—and yet they have made

[1]cochineal –red dye made from a South American insect

[2]p—x—d–poxed; afflicted with venereal disease

cannons and bayonets to destroy one another. Into this account I might throw not only bankrupts, but Justice which seizes on the effects of bankrupts to cheat the creditors."

"All this was indispensable," replied the one-eyed doctor, "for private misfortunes make the general good, so that the more private misfortunes there are the greater is the general good."

While he reasoned, the sky darkened, the winds blew from the four quarters, and the ship was assailed by a most terrible tempest.

## Questions:

1. What is the difference between James' and Pangloss' philosophy?

2. Where did Paquette get the venereal disease that she eventually gave to Pangloss? Why is this ironic?

## Essay/Discussion Question:

What does Pangloss say about private misfortunes? Do you agree with this? Explain your opinion in a few paragraphs.

# Mark Twain (Samuel Longhorne Clemens)

Twain (1835-1910) is still considered one of the greatest American novelists and humorists. In *The Adventures of Huckleberry Finn*, he satirizes almost every aspect of American life, from politics to religion to race relations. As his mouthpiece, he uses a boy named Huckleberry Finn, who speaks in the vernacular—rough, "improper" English as opposed to formal, grammatical English. Huck's total honesty allows Twain to point out some things that adult readers might otherwise refuse to see, such as the unfairness of slavery and the cruel things done by people who consider themselves good Christians.

Literary trends are also a target. In the last quarter of the nineteenth century, Gothic novels were extremely popular in the United States and England. These were romantic works that focused on horror or tragedy; the writings of Edgar Allen Poe are a famous example. In the excerpt below, as Huck recalls the time he spent with a family called the Grangerfords, Twain takes aim at the mournful side of Gothic literature.

### *from The Adventures of Huckleberry Finn*

### Chapter 17

THEY HAD PICTURES hung on the walls–mainly Washingtons and Lafayettes,[1] and battles, and Highland Marys,[2] and one called "Signing the Declaration." There was some that they called crayons, which one of the daughters which was dead made her own self when she was only fifteen years old. They was different from any pictures I ever see before—blacker, mostly, than is common. One was a woman in a slim black dress,belted small under the armpits, with bulges like a cabbage in the middle of the sleeves, and a large black scoop-shovel bonnet with a black veil, and white slim ankles crossed about with black tape, and very wee black slippers, like a chisel, and she was leaning pensive on a tombstone on her right elbow, under a weeping willow, and her other hand hanging down her side holding a white handkerchief and a reticule, and underneath the picture it said "Shall I Never See Thee More Alas." Another one was a young lady with her hair all combed up straight to the top of her head, and knotted there in front of a comb like a chair-back, and she was crying into a handkerchief and had a dead bird laying on its back in her other hand with its heels up, and underneath the

[1]Lafayette–French general who led forces against the British in the American
    Revolutionary War
[2]Highland Marys–Romantic paintings of a Scottish maiden; common decorations
    in houses of the time

picture it said "I Shall Never Hear Thy Sweet Chirrup More Alas." There was one where a young lady was at a window looking up at the moon, and tears running down her cheeks; and she had an open letter in one hand with black sealing wax showing on one edge of it, and she was mashing a locket with a chain to it against her mouth, and underneath the picture it said "And Art Thou Gone Yes Thou Art Gone Alas." These was all nice pictures, I reckon, but I didn't somehow seem to take to them, because if ever I was down a little they always give me the fan-tods.[3] Everybody was sorry she died, because she had laid out a lot more of these pictures to do, and a body could see by what she had done what they had lost. But I reckoned that with her disposition she was having a better time in the graveyard. She was at work on what they said was her greatest picture when she took sick, and every day and every night it was her prayer to be allowed to live till she got it done, but she never got the chance. It was a picture of a young woman in a long white gown, standing on the rail of a bridge all ready to jump off, with her hair all down her back, and looking up to the moon, with the tears running down her face, and she had two arms folded across her breast, and two arms stretched out in front, and two more reaching up towards the moon—and the idea was to see which pair would look best, and then scratch out all the other arms; but, as I was saying, she died before she got her mind made up, and now they kept this picture over the head of the bed in her room, and every time her birthday come they hung flowers on it. Other times it was hid with a little curtain. The young woman in the picture had a kind of a nice sweet face, but there was so many arms it made her look too spidery, seemed to me.

This young girl kept a scrap-book when she was alive, and used to paste obituaries and accidents and cases of patient suffering in it out of the Presbyterian Observer, and write poetry after them out of her own head. It was very good poetry. This is what she wrote about a boy by the name of Stephen Dowling Bots that fell down a well and was drownded:

### ODE TO STEPHEN DOWLING BOTS, DEC'D

> And did young Stephen sicken,
> And did young Stephen die?
>  And did the sad hearts thicken,
> And did the mourners cry?
>
> No; such was not the fate of
> Young Stephen Dowling Bots;
> Though sad hearts round him thickened,
> 'Twas not from sickness' shots.

[3]fan-tods—creeps

No whooping-cough did rack his frame,
Nor measles drear with spots;
Not these impaired the sacred name
Of Stephen Dowling Bots.

Despised love struck not with woe
That head of curly knots,
Nor stomach troubles laid him low,
Young Stephen Dowling Bots.

O no.  Then list with tearful eye,
 Whilst I his fate do tell.
His soul did from this cold world fly
By falling down a well.

They got him out and emptied him;
Alas it was too late;
His spirit was gone for to sport aloft
 In the realms of the good and great.

If Emmeline Grangerford could make poetry like that before she was fourteen, there ain't no telling what she could a done by and by.  Buck said she could rattle off poetry like nothing.  She didn't ever have to stop to think.  He said she would slap down a line, and if she couldn't find anything to rhyme with it would just scratch it out and slap down another one, and go ahead.  She warn't particular; she could write about anything you choose to give her to write about just so it was sadful.  Every time a man died, or a woman died, or a child died, she would be on hand with her "tribute" before he was cold.  She called them tributes.  The neighbors said it was the doctor first, then Emmeline, then the undertaker—the undertaker never got in ahead of Emmeline but once, and then she hung fire on a rhyme for the dead person's name, which was Whistler.  She warn't ever the same after that; she never complained, but she kinder pined away and did not live long.  Poor thing, many's the time I made myself go up to the little room that used to be hers and get out her poor old scrap-book and read in it when her pictures had been aggravating me and I had soured on her a little.  I liked all that family, dead ones and all, and warn't going to let anything come between us. Poor Emmeline made poetry about all the dead people when she was alive, and it didn't seem right that there warn't nobody to make some about her now she was gone; so I tried to sweat out a verse or two myself, but I couldn't seem to make it go somehow.

**Questions:**

1. What do you notice about the titles of the crayon drawings? What point is Twain making?

2. What kind of language does Huck use to describe the figures in the paintings? Do you think Emmeline Grangerford would describe them the same way?

3. Describe Emmeline's poetry. What kinds of rhyme does she use? Is her language simple or exaggerated?

4. What does Huck say about Emmeline's poetry? Do you think Twain feels the same way?

# Saki (H.H. Munroe)

"Saki" was the pen name of the British writer H.H. Munroe (1870-1916). His stories mocked the values and social habits of early 20th-century England.

## The Schartz-Metterklume Method

LADY CARLOTTA STEPPED out on to the platform of the small wayside station and took a turn or two up and down its uninteresting length, to kill time till the train should be pleased to proceed on its way. Then, in the roadway beyond, she saw a horse struggling with a more than ample load, and a carter[1] of the sort that seems to bear a sullen hatred against the animal that helps him to earn a living. Lady Carlotta promptly betook her to the roadway, and put rather a different complexion on the struggle. Certain of her acquaintances were wont to give her plentiful warning as to the undesirability of interfering on behalf of a distressed animal, such interference being "none of her business." Only once had she put the doctrine of non-interference into practice, when one of its most eloquent exponents had been besieged for nearly three hours in a small and extremely uncomfortable tree by an angry boar-pig, while Lady Carlotta, on the other side of the fence, had proceeded with the water-colour sketch she was engaged on, and refused to interfere between the boar and his prisoner. It is to be feared that she lost the friendship of the ultimately rescued lady. On this occasion she merely lost the train, which gave way to the worst sign of impatience it had shown throughout the journey, and steamed off without her. She bore the desertion with philosophical indifference; her friends and relations were thoroughly well used to the fact of her luggage arriving without her. She wired a vague noncommittal message to her destination to say that she was coming on "by another train." Before she had time to think what her next move might be, she was confronted by an imposingly attired lady, who seemed to be taking a prolonged mental inventory of her clothes and looks.

"You must be Miss Hope, the governess I've come to meet," said the apparition, in a tone that admitted of very little argument.

"Very well, if I must I must," said Lady Carlotta to herself with dangerous meekness.

"I am Mrs. Quabarl," continued the lady; "and where, pray, is your luggage?"

"It's gone astray," said the alleged governess, falling in with the excellent rule of life that the absent are always to blame; the luggage had, in point of fact,

---

[1]carter—traveling tradesman

behaved with perfect correctitude. "I've just telegraphed about it," she added, with a nearer approach to truth.

"How provoking," said Mrs. Quabarl; "these railway companies are so careless. However, my maid can lend you things for the night," and she led the way to her car.

While driving to the Quabarl mansion Lady Carlotta was impressively introduced to the nature of the charge that had been thrust upon her; she learned that Claude and Wilfrid were delicate, sensitive young people, that Irene had the artistic temperament highly developed, and that Viola was something or other else of a mold equally commonplace among children of that class and type in the twentieth century.

"I wish them not only to be taught," said Mrs. Quabarl, "but interested in what they learn. In their history lessons, for instance, you must try to make them feel that they are being introduced to the life-stories of men and women who really lived, not merely committing a mass of names and dates to memory. French, of course, I shall expect you to talk at mealtimes several days in the week."

"I shall talk French four days of the week and Russian in the remaining three."

"Russian? My dear Miss Hope, no one in the house speaks or understands Russian."

"That will not embarrass me in the least," said Lady Carlotta coldly.

Mrs. Quabarl, to use a colloquial expression, was knocked off her perch. She was one of those imperfectly self-assured individuals who are magnificent and autocratic[2] as long as they are not seriously opposed. The least show of unexpected resistance goes a long way towards rendering them cowed and apologetic. When the new governess failed to express wondering admiration of the large newly purchased and expensive car, and lightly alluded to the superior advantages of one or two makes which had just been put on the market, the unease of her patroness became almost abject. Her feelings were those which might have animated a general of ancient warfaring days, on beholding his heaviest battle-elephant ignominiously driven off the field by slingers and javelin throwers.

At dinner that evening, although reinforced by her husband, who usually duplicated her opinions and lent her moral support generally, Mrs. Quabarl regained none of her lost ground. The governess not only helped herself well and truly to wine, but held forth with considerable show of critical knowledge on various vintage matters, concerning which the Quabarl were in no wise able to pose as authorities. Previous governesses had limited their conversation on the wine topic to a respectful and doubtless sincere expression of a preference

[2]autocratic–having total power over others

for water. When this one went as far as to recommend a wine firm in whose hands you could not go very far wrong Mrs. Quabarl thought it time to turn the conversation into more usual channels.

"We got very satisfactory references about you from Canon Teep," she observed, "a very estimable[3] man, I should think."

"Drinks like a fish and beats his wife, otherwise a very lovable character," said the governess imperturbably.[4]

"My dear Miss Hope! I trust you are exaggerating," exclaimed the Quabarl in unison.

"One must in justice admit that there is some provocation," continued the romancer. "Mrs. Teep is quite the most irritating bridge-player that I have ever sat down with, her leads and declarations[5] would condone a certain amount of brutality in her partner, but to souse her with the contents of the only soda-water siphon in the house on a Sunday afternoon, when one couldn't get another, argues an indifference to the comfort of others which I cannot altogether overlook. You may think me hasty in my judgments, but it was practically on account of the siphon[6] incident that I left."

"We will talk of this some other time," said Mrs. Quabarl hastily.

"I shall never allude to it again," said the governess with decision.

Mr. Quabarl made a welcome diversion by asking what studies the new instructors proposed to inaugurate on the morrow.

"History to begin with," she informed him.

"Ah, history," he observed sagely; "now in teaching them history you must take care to interest them in what they learn. You must make them feel that they are being introduced to the life-stories of men and women who really lived."

"I've told her all that," interposed Mrs. Quabarl.

"I teach history on the Schartz-Metterklume method," said the governess loftily.

"Ah, yes," said her listeners, thinking it expedient to assume an acquaintance at least with the name.

\*\*\*

"What are you children doing out here?" demanded Mrs. Quabarl the next morning, on finding Irene sitting rather glumly at the head of the stairs, while her sister was perched in an attitude of depressed discomfort on the window-seat behind her, with a wolf-skin rug almost covering her.

[3]estimable–deserving respect
[4]imperturbably–calmly
[5]leads and declarations–moves in the game of bridge
[6]siphon–a bottle for carbonated water

"We are having a history lesson," came the unexpected reply. "I am supposed to be Rome, and Viola up there is the she-wolf, not a real wolf but the figure of one that the Romans used to set store by—I forget why. Claude and Wilfrid have gone to fetch the shabby[7] women."

"The shabby women?"

"Yes, they've got to carry them off. They didn't want to, but Miss Hope got one of father's fives-bats[8] and said she'd give them a number nine spanking if they didn't, so they've gone to do it."

A loud, angry screaming from the direction of the lawn drew Mrs. Quabarl thither in hot haste, fearful lest the threatened beating might even now be in process of infliction. The outcry, however, came principally from the two small daughters of the lodge-keeper, who were being hauled and pushed towards the house by the panting and disheveled Claude and Wilfrid, whose task was rendered even more difficult by the incessant, if not very effectual, attacks of the captured maidens' small brother. The governess, fives-bat in hand, sat negligently on the stone wall, presiding over the scene with the cold impartiality of a Goddess of Battles. A furious and repeated chorus of "I'll tell mother" rose from the lodge children, but the lodge-mother, who was hard of hearing, was for the moment immersed in the preoccupation of her washtub. After an apprehensive glance in the direction of the lodge (the good woman was gifted with the highly militant temper which is sometimes the privilege of deafness) Mrs. Quabarl flew indignantly to the rescue of the struggling captives.

"Wilfrid! Claude! Let those children go at once. Miss Hope, what on earth is the meaning of this scene?"

"Early Roman history; the Sabine women, don't you know? It's the Schartz-Metterklume method to make children understand history by acting it themselves; fixes it in their memory, you know. Of course, if thanks to your interference, your boys go through life thinking that the Sabine women ultimately escaped, I really cannot be held responsible."

"You may be very clever and modern, Miss Hope," said Mrs. Quabarl firmly, "but I should like you to leave here by the next train. Your luggage will be sent after you as soon as it arrives."

"I'm not certain exactly where I shall be for the next few days,' said the dismissed instructress of youth; 'you might keep my luggage till I wire my address. There are only a couple of trunks and some golf-clubs and a leopard cub."

"A leopard cub!" gasped Mrs. Quabarl. Even in her departure this extraordinary person seemed destined to leave a trail of embarrassment behind her.

---

[7]shabby—mistake for *Sabine*. According to Roman legend, the first men in Rome had
  no wives, so they kidnapped women from a tribe called the Sabines.
[8]fives-bat—bat used in a game similar to racquetball

"Well, it's rather left off being a cub; it's more than half-grown, you know. A fowl every day and a rabbit on Sundays is what it usually gets. Raw beef makes it too excitable. Don't trouble about getting the car for me, I'm rather inclined for a walk."

And Lady Carlotta strode out of the Quabarl horizon.

The arrival of the genuine Miss Hope, who had made a mistake as to the day on which she was due to arrive, caused a turmoil which that good lady was quite unused to inspiring. Obviously the Quabarl family had been woefully befooled, but a certain amount of relief came with the knowledge.

"How tiresome for you, dear Carlotta," said her hostess, when the overdue guest ultimately arrived; "how very tiresome losing your train and having to stop overnight in a strange place."

"Oh, dear, no," said Lady Carlotta; "not at all tiresome—for me."

## Questions:

1. The Quabarls want their children to "feel that they are being introduced to the life-stories of men and women who really lived." How does Lady Carlotta treat this idea?

2. Are the children, from what we see of them, the way Mrs. Quabarl describes them to Lady Carlotta?

3. What one word would you use to describe the narrator's tone in this story? Give some words and phrases that support your answer.

4. Is the target of this satire a specific individual or a type of person? How do you know?

# Sinclair Lewis

Sinclair Lewis (1885-1951) wrote both novels and plays. *Babbitt* (1922) is set in the fictional state of Winnemac, which Lewis created to resemble other midwestern states. Zenith, the city George Babbitt mentions, is the capital of Winnemac; both the town and state are seeing economic growth and the development of new real estate.

In this scene, we get our first glimpse of Babbitt, a real-estate salesman, and his wife, Myra.

## from *Babbitt*, Chapter 1

THERE IS CHARACTER in spectacles—the pretentious tortoiseshell, the meek pince-nez[1] of the school teacher, the twisted silver-framed glasses of the old villager. Babbitt's spectacles had huge, circular, frameless lenses of the very best glass; the ear-pieces were thin bars of gold. In them he was the modern business man; one who gave orders to clerks and drove a car and played occasional golf and was scholarly in regard to Salesmanship. His head suddenly appeared not babyish but weighty, and you noted his heavy, blunt nose, his straight mouth and thick, long upper lip, his chin overfleshy but strong; with respect you beheld him put on the rest of his uniform as a Solid Citizen.

The gray suit was well cut, well made, and completely undistinguished. It was a standard suit. White piping on the V of the vest added a flavor of law and learning. His shoes were black laced boots, good boots, honest boots, standard boots, extraordinarily uninteresting boots. The only frivolity was in his purple knitted scarf. With considerable comment on the matter to Mrs. Babbitt (who, acrobatically fastening the back of her blouse to her skirt with a safety-pin, did not hear a word he said), he chose between the purple scarf and a tapestry effect with stringless brown harps among blown palms, and into it he thrust a snake-head pin with opal eyes.

A sensational event was changing from the brown suit to the gray the contents of his pockets. He was earnest about these objects. They were of eternal importance, like baseball or the Republican Party. They included a fountain pen and a silver pencil (always lacking a supply of new leads) which belonged in the righthand upper vest pocket. Without them he would have felt naked. On his watch-chain were a gold penknife, silver cigar-cutter, seven keys (the use of two of which he had forgotten), and incidentally a good watch. Depending from the chain was a large, yellowish elk's-tooth-proclamation of his membership in the Brotherly and Protective Order of Elks. Most significant of all was his loose-

---

[1]pince-nez–literally, "pinch-nose"; eyeglasses with small frames

leaf pocket note-book, that modern and efficient note-book which contained the addresses of people whom he had forgotten, prudent memoranda of postal money-orders which had reached their destinations months ago, stamps which had lost their mucilage,[2] clippings of verses by T. Cholmondeley Frink and of the newspaper editorials from which Babbitt got his opinions and his polysyllables, notes to be sure and do things which he did not intend to do, and one curious inscription—D.S.S.D.M.Y.P.D.F.

But he had no cigarette-case. No one had ever happened to give him one, so he hadn't the habit, and people who carried cigarette-cases he regarded as effeminate.

Last, he stuck in his lapel the Boosters' Club[3] button. With the conciseness of great art the button displayed two words: "Boosters-Pep!" It made Babbitt feel loyal and important. It associated him with Good Fellows, with men who were nice and human, and important in business circles. It was his V.C., his Legion of Honor ribbon, his Phi Beta Kappa key.

With the subtleties of dressing ran other complex worries. "I feel kind of punk[4] this morning," he said. "I think I had too much dinner last evening. You oughtn't to serve those heavy banana fritters."

"But you asked me to have some."

"I know, but—I tell you, when a fellow gets past forty he has to look after his digestion. There's a lot of fellows that don't take proper care of themselves. I tell you at forty a man's a fool or his doctor—I mean, his own doctor. Folks don't give enough attention to this matter of dieting. Now I think—Course a man ought to have a good meal after the day's work, but it would be a good thing for both of us if we took lighter lunches."

"But Georgie, here at home I always do have a light lunch."

"Mean to imply I make a hog of myself, eating down-town? Yes, sure! You'd have a swell time if you had to eat the truck that new steward hands out to us at the Athletic Club! But I certainly do feel out of sorts, this morning. Funny, got a pain down here on the left side—but no, that wouldn't be appendicitis, would it? Last night, when I was driving over to Verg Gunch's, I felt a pain in my stomach, too. Right here it was--kind of a sharp shooting pain. I—Where'd that dime go to? Why don't you serve more prunes at breakfast? Of course I eat an apple every evening—an apple a day keeps the doctor away—but still, you ought to have more prunes, and not all these fancy doodads."

"The last time I had prunes you didn't eat them."

"Well, I didn't feel like eating 'em, I suppose. Matter of fact, I think I did eat some of 'em. Anyway—I tell you it's mighty important to—I was saying to Verg Gunch, just last evening, most people don't take sufficient care of their diges—"

[2]mucilage–glue
[3]Booster's Club–an organization formed to promote a town or civic organization.
[4]punk–ill

"Shall we have the Gunches for our dinner, next week?"

"Why sure; you bet."

"Now see here, George: I want you to put on your nice dinner-jacket that evening."

"Rats! The rest of 'em won't want to dress."

"Of course they will. You remember when you didn't dress for the Littlefields' supper-party, and all the rest did, and how embarrassed you were."

"Embarrassed, hell! I wasn't embarrassed. Everybody knows I can put on as expensive a Tux. as anybody else, and I should worry if I don't happen to have it on sometimes. All a darn nuisance, anyway. All right for a woman, that stays around the house all the time, but when a fellow's worked like the dickens all day, he doesn't want to go and hustle his head off getting into the soup-and-fish for a lot of folks that he's seen in just reg'lar ordinary clothes that same day."

"You know you enjoy being seen in one. The other evening you admitted you were glad I'd insisted on your dressing. You said you felt a lot better for it. And oh, Georgie, I do wish you wouldn't say 'Tux.' It's 'dinner-jacket.'"

"Rats, what's the odds?"

"Well, it's what all the nice folks say. Suppose Lucile McKelvey heard you calling it a 'Tux.'"

"Well, that's all right now! Lucile McKelvey can't pull anything on me! Her folks are common as mud, even if her husband and her dad are millionaires! I suppose you're trying to rub in your exalted social position! Well, let me tell you that your revered paternal ancestor, Henry T., doesn't even call it a 'Tux.'! He calls it a 'bobtail jacket for a ringtail monkey,' and you couldn't get him into one unless you chloroformed him!"

"Now don't be horrid, George."

"Well, I don't want to be horrid, but Lord! you're getting as fussy as Verona. Ever since she got out of college she's been too rambunctious to live with—doesn't know what she wants—well, I know what she wants!—all she wants is to marry a millionaire, and live in Europe, and hold some preacher's hand, and simultaneously at the same time stay right here in Zenith and be some blooming kind of a socialist agitator or boss charity-worker or some damn thing! Lord, and Ted is just as bad! He wants to go to college, and he doesn't want to go to college. Only one of the three that knows her own mind is Tinka. Simply can't understand how I ever came to have a pair of shillyshallying children like Rone and Ted. I may not be any Rockefeller or James J. Shakespeare, but I certainly do know my own mind, and I do keep right on plugging along in the office and—Do you know the latest? Far as I can figure out, Ted's new bee is he'd like to be a movie actor and—And here I've told him a hundred times, if he'll go to college and law-school and make good, I'll set him up in business and—Verona just exactly as bad. Doesn't know what she wants. Well, well, come on! Aren't you ready yet? The girl rang the bell three minutes ago."

\*\*\*

Before he followed his wife, Babbitt stood at the westernmost window of their room.  This residential settlement, Floral Heights, was on a rise; and though the center of the city was three miles away–Zenith had between three and four hundred thousand inhabitants now–he could see the top of the Second National Tower, an Indiana limestone building of thirty-five stories.

Its shining walls rose against April sky to a simple cornice like a streak of white fire.  Integrity was in the tower, and decision. It bore its strength lightly as a tall soldier.  As Babbitt stared, the nervousness was soothed from his face, his slack chin lifted in reverence.  All he articulated was "That's one lovely sight!" but he was inspired by the rhythm of the city; his love of it renewed. He beheld the tower as a temple-spire of the religion of business, a faith passionate, exalted, surpassing common men; and as he clumped down to breakfast he whistled the ballad "Oh, by gee, by gosh, by jingo" as though it were a hymn melancholy and noble.

## Questions:

1.  Why does Lewis capitalize the phrase "Solid Citizen"?

2.  Why doesn't Babbitt have a cigarette case?

3.  What does Lewis say about Babbitt's boots? What is the effect of this language?

4.  What or who is the target of this satire?

5.  List some words that you think are used ironically in this passage.

# CHAPTER V
## SATIRICAL ESSAYS

# Jonathan Swift

## A Modest Proposal

PREVENTING THE CHILDREN OF POOR PEOPLE IN IRELAND FROM
BEING A BURDEN TO THEIR PARENTS OR COUNTRY, AND FOR MAKING
THEM BENEFICIAL TO THE PUBLIC

IT IS A MELANCHOLY object to those, who walk through this great town,
or travel in the country, when they see the streets, the roads and cabin-doors
crowded with beggars of the female sex, followed by three, four, or six children,
all in rags, and importuning every passenger for an alms. These mothers instead
of being able to work for their honest livelihood, are forced to employ all their
time in strolling to beg sustenance for their helpless infants who, as they grow up,
either turn thieves for want of work, or leave their dear native country, to fight for
the Pretender[1] in Spain, or sell themselves to the Barbadoes.[2]

I think it is agreed by all parties, that this prodigious[3] number of children in
the arms, or on the backs, or at the heels of their mothers, and frequently of their
fathers, is in the present deplorable state of the kingdom, a very great additional
grievance; and therefore whoever could find out a fair, cheap and easy method of
making these children sound and useful members of the common-wealth, would
deserve so well of the publick, as to have his statue set up for a preserver of
the nation.

But my intention is very far from being confined to provide only for the
children of professed beggars: it is of a much greater extent, and shall take in the
whole number of infants at a certain age, who are born of parents in effect as little

[1]Pretender–James Francis Edward Stuart, son of James VII of England and II of Scotland;
    instead of taking the throne, he had been forced to leave the country.
[2]Barbadoes–pirates from the northern coast of Africa
[3]prodigious–very great

able to support them, as those who demand our charity in the streets.

As to my own part, having turned my thoughts for many years, upon this important subject, and maturely weighed the several schemes of our projectors, I have always found them grossly mistaken in their computation. It is true, a child just dropt from its dam,[4] may be supported by her milk, for a solar year, with little other nourishment: at most not above the value of two shillings,[5] which the mother may certainly get, or the value in scraps, by her lawful occupation of begging; and it is exactly at one year old that I propose to provide for them in such a manner, as, instead of being a charge upon their parents, or the parish, or wanting food and raiment[6] for the rest of their lives, they shall, on the contrary, contribute to the feeding, and partly to the cloathing of many thousands.

There is likewise another great advantage in my scheme, that it will prevent those voluntary abortions, and that horrid practice of women murdering their bastard children, alas! too frequent among us, sacrificing the poor innocent babes, I doubt, more to avoid the expence than the shame, which would move tears and pity in the most savage and inhuman breast.

The number of souls in this kingdom being usually reckoned one million and a half, of these I calculate there may be about two hundred thousand couple whose wives are breeders; from which number I subtract thirty thousand couple, who are able to maintain their own children, (although I apprehend there cannot be so many, under the present distresses of the kingdom) but this being granted, there will remain an hundred and seventy thousand breeders. I again subtract fifty thousand, for those women who miscarry, or whose children die by accident or disease within the year. There only remain an hundred and twenty thousand children of poor parents annually born. The question therefore is, How this number shall be reared, and provided for? which, as I have already said, under the present situation of affairs, is utterly impossible by all the methods hitherto proposed. For we can neither employ them in handicraft or agriculture; we neither build houses, (I mean in the country) nor cultivate land: they can very seldom pick up a livelihood by stealing till they arrive at six years old; except where they are of towardly[7] parts, although I confess they learn the rudiments much earlier; during which time they can however be properly looked upon only as probationers: As I have been informed by a principal gentleman in the county of Cavan, who protested to me, that he never knew above one or two instances under the age of six, even in a part of the kingdom so renowned for the quickest proficiency in that art.

I am assured by our merchants, that a boy or a girl before twelve years old, is

[4]dam–mother
[5]shillings–small coins
[6]raiment–garment
[7]towardly–easy to teach

no saleable commodity, and even when they come to this age, they will not yield above three pounds,[8] or three pounds and half a crown[9] at most, on the exchange; which cannot turn to account either to the parents or kingdom, the charge of nutriments and rags having been at least four times that value.

I shall now therefore humbly propose my own thoughts, which I hope will not be liable to the least objection.

I have been assured by a very knowing American of my acquaintance in London, that a young healthy child well nursed, is, at a year old, a most delicious nourishing and wholesome food, whether stewed, roasted, baked, or boiled; and I make no doubt that it will equally serve in a fricasie,[10] or a ragoust.[11]

I do therefore humbly offer it to publick consideration, that of the hundred and twenty thousand children, already computed, twenty thousand may be reserved for breed, whereof only one fourth part to be males; which is more than we allow to sheep, black cattle, or swine, and my reason is, that these children are seldom the fruits of marriage, a circumstance not much regarded by our savages, therefore, one male will be sufficient to serve four females. That the remaining hundred thousand may, at a year old, be offered in sale to the persons of quality and fortune, through the kingdom, always advising the mother to let them suck plentifully in the last month, so as to render them plump, and fat for a good table. A child will make two dishes at an entertainment for friends, and when the family dines alone, the fore or hind quarter will make a reasonable dish, and seasoned with a little pepper or salt, will be very good boiled on the fourth day, especially in winter.

I have reckoned upon a medium, that a child just born will weigh 12 pounds, and in a solar year, if tolerably nursed, encreaseth to 28 pounds.

I grant this food will be somewhat dear, and therefore very proper for landlords, who, as they have already devoured most of the parents, seem to have the best title to the children.

Infant's flesh will be in season throughout the year, but more plentiful in March, and a little before and after; for we are told by a grave author, an eminent French physician, that fish being a prolific diet, there are more children born in Roman Catholic countries about nine months after Lent,[12] the markets will be more glutted than usual, because the number of Popish infants, is at least three to one in this kingdom, and therefore it will have one other collateral advantage, by lessening the number of Papists among us.

I have already computed the charge of nursing a beggar's child (in which list

---

[8]pounds—coins worth twenty shillings

[9]crowns—coins worth five shillings

[10]fricasie—dish made of fried meat served in gravy

[11]ragoust—stew

[12]Lent—period before the Christian holiday of Easter; Catholics are supposed to eat fish, but not meat, during Lent

I reckon all cottagers, labourers, and four-fifths of the farmers) to be about two shillings per annum, rags included; and I believe no gentleman would repine to give ten shillings for the carcass of a good fat child, which, as I have said, will make four dishes of excellent nutritive meat, when he hath only some particular friend, or his own family to dine with him. Thus the squire will learn to be a good landlord, and grow popular among his tenants, the mother will have eight shillings neat profit, and be fit for work till she produces another child.

Those who are more thrifty (as I must confess the times require) may flea the carcass; the skin of which, artificially dressed, will make admirable gloves for ladies, and summer boots for fine gentlemen.

As to our City of Dublin, shambles may be appointed for this purpose, in the most convenient parts of it, and butchers we may be assured will not be wanting; although I rather recommend buying the children alive, and dressing them hot from the knife, as we do roasting pigs.

A very worthy person, a true lover of his country, and whose virtues I highly esteem, was lately pleased, in discoursing on this matter, to offer a refinement upon my scheme. He said, that many gentlemen of this kingdom, having of late destroyed their deer, he conceived that the want of venison might be well supply'd by the bodies of young lads and maidens, not exceeding fourteen years of age, nor under twelve; so great a number of both sexes in every country being now ready to starve for want of work and service: And these to be disposed of by their parents if alive, or otherwise by their nearest relations. But with due deference to so excellent a friend, and so deserving a patriot, I cannot be altogether in his sentiments; for as to the males, my American acquaintance assured me from frequent experience, that their flesh was generally tough and lean, like that of our school-boys, by continual exercise, and their taste disagreeable, and to fatten them would not answer the charge. Then as to the females, it would, I think, with humble submission, be a loss to the public, because they soon would become breeders themselves: And besides, it is not improbable that some scrupulous people might be apt to censure such a practice, (although indeed very unjustly) as a little bordering upon cruelty, which, I confess, hath always been with me the strongest objection against any project, how well soever intended.

But in order to justify my friend, he confessed, that this expedient was put into his head by the famous Salmanaazor, a native of the island Formosa, who came from thence to London, above twenty years ago, and in conversation told my friend, that in his country, when any young person happened to be put to death, the executioner sold the carcass to persons of quality, as a prime dainty; and that, in his time, the body of a plump girl of fifteen, who was crucified for an attempt to poison the Emperor, was sold to his imperial majesty's prime minister of state, and other great mandarins[13] of the court in joints from the gibbet,[14]

[13]mandarins—officials
[14]gibbet—gallows

at four hundred crowns. Neither indeed can I deny, that if the same use were made of several plump young girls in this town, who without one single groat to their fortunes, cannot stir abroad without a chair, and appear at a play-house and assemblies in foreign fineries which they never will pay for; the kingdom would not be the worse.

Some persons of a desponding spirit are in great concern about that vast number of poor people, who are aged, diseased, or maimed; and I have been desired to employ my thoughts what course may be taken, to ease the nation of so grievous an incumbrance. But I am not in the least pain upon that matter, because it is very well known, that they are every day dying, and rotting, by cold and famine, and filth, and vermin, as fast as can be reasonably expected. And as to the young labourers, they are now in almost as hopeful a condition. They cannot get work, and consequently pine away from want of nourishment, to a degree, that if at any time they are accidentally hired to common labour, they have not strength to perform it, and thus the country and themselves are happily delivered from the evils to come.

I have too long digressed, and therefore shall return to my subject. I think the advantages by the proposal which I have made are obvious and many, as well as of the highest importance.

For first, as I have already observed, it would greatly lessen the number of Papists, with whom we are yearly over-run, being the principal breeders of the nation, as well as our most dangerous enemies, and who stay at home on purpose with a design to deliver the kingdom to the Pretender, hoping to take their advantage by the absence of so many good Protestants, who have chosen rather to leave their country, than stay at home and pay tithes[15] against their conscience to an episcopal curate.[16]

Secondly, The poorer tenants will have something valuable of their own, which by law may be made liable to a distress, and help to pay their landlord's rent, their corn and cattle being already seized, and money a thing unknown.

Thirdly, Whereas the maintainance of an hundred thousand children, from two years old, and upwards, cannot be computed at less than ten shillings a piece per annum, the nation's stock will be thereby encreased fifty thousand pounds per annum, besides the profit of a new dish, introduced to the tables of all gentlemen of fortune in the kingdom, who have any refinement in taste. And the money will circulate among our selves, the goods being entirely of our own growth and manufacture.

[15]tithes–church dues
[16]curate–priest

Fourthly, The constant breeders, besides the gain of eight shillings sterling[17] per annum[18] by the sale of their children, will be rid of the charge of maintaining them after the first year.

Fifthly, This food would likewise bring great custom to taverns, where the vintners[19] will certainly be so prudent as to procure the best receipts for dressing it to perfection; and consequently have their houses frequented by all the fine gentlemen, who justly value themselves upon their knowledge in good eating; and a skilful cook, who understands how to oblige his guests, will contrive to make it as expensive as they please.

Sixthly, This would be a great inducement to marriage, which all wise nations have either encouraged by rewards, or enforced by laws and penalties. It would encrease the care and tenderness of mothers towards their children, when they were sure of a settlement for life to the poor babes, provided in some sort by the public, to their annual profit instead of expence. We should soon see an honest emulation among the married women, which of them could bring the fattest child to the market. Men would become as fond of their wives, during the time of their pregnancy, as they are now of their mares in foal, their cows in calf, or sow when they are ready to farrow; nor offer to beat or kick them (as is too frequent a practice) for fear of a miscarriage.

Many other advantages might be enumerated. For instance, the addition of some thousand carcasses in our exportation of barrel'd beef: the propagation of swine's flesh, and improvement in the art of making good bacon, so much wanted among us by the great destruction of pigs, too frequent at our tables; which are no way comparable in taste or magnificence to a well grown, fat yearly child, which roasted whole will make a considerable figure at a Lord Mayor's feast, or any other publick entertainment. But this, and many others, I omit, being studious of brevity.

Supposing that one thousand families in this city, would be constant customers for infants flesh, besides others who might have it at merry meetings, particularly at weddings and christenings, I compute that Dublin would take off annually about twenty thousand carcasses; and the rest of the kingdom (where probably they will be sold somewhat cheaper) the remaining eighty thousand.

I can think of no one objection, that will possibly be raised against this proposal, unless it should be urged, that the number of people will be thereby much lessened in the kingdom. This I freely own, and 'twas indeed one principal design in offering it to the world. I desire the reader will observe, that I calculate my remedy for this one individual Kingdom of Ireland, and for no other that ever was, is, or, I think, ever can be upon Earth. Therefore let no man talk to me of other expedients: Of taxing our absentees at five shillings a pound: Of using

[17]sterling–sterling silver, a sign that the coins have the value they claim to
[18]per annum–per year
[19]vintner–wine-merchant

neither clothes, nor houshold furniture, except what is of our own growth and manufacture: Of utterly rejecting the materials and instruments that promote foreign luxury: Of curing the expensiveness of pride, vanity, idleness, and gaming in our women: Of introducing a vein of parsimony, prudence and temperance: Of learning to love our country, wherein we differ even from Laplanders, and the inhabitants of Topinamboo: Of quitting our animosities and factions, nor acting any longer like the Jews, who were murdering one another at the very moment their city was taken: Of being a little cautious not to sell our country and consciences for nothing: Of teaching landlords to have at least one degree of mercy towards their tenants. Lastly, of putting a spirit of honesty, industry, and skill into our shop-keepers, who, if a resolution could now be taken to buy only our native goods, would immediately unite to cheat and exact upon us in the price, the measure, and the goodness, nor could ever yet be brought to make one fair proposal of just dealing, though often and earnestly invited to it.

Therefore I repeat, let no man talk to me of these and the like expedients, 'till he hath at least some glympse of hope, that there will ever be some hearty and sincere attempt to put them into practice.

But, as to my self, having been wearied out for many years with offering vain, idle, visionary thoughts, and at length utterly despairing of success, I fortunately fell upon this proposal, which, as it is wholly new, so it hath something solid and real, of no expence and little trouble, full in our own power, and whereby we can incur no danger in disobliging England. For this kind of commodity will not bear exportation, and flesh being of too tender a consistence, to admit a long continuance in salt, although perhaps I could name a country, which would be glad to eat up our whole nation without it.

After all, I am not so violently bent upon my own opinion, as to reject any offer, proposed by wise men, which shall be found equally innocent, cheap, easy, and effectual. But before something of that kind shall be advanced in contradiction to my scheme, and offering a better, I desire the author or authors will be pleased maturely to consider two points. First, As things now stand, how they will be able to find food and raiment for a hundred thousand useless mouths and backs. And secondly, There being a round million of creatures in humane figure throughout this kingdom, whose whole subsistence put into a common stock, would leave them in debt two million of pounds sterling, adding those who are beggars by profession, to the bulk of farmers, cottagers and labourers, with their wives and children, who are beggars in effect; I desire those politicians who dislike my overture, and may perhaps be so bold to attempt an answer, that they will first ask the parents of these mortals, whether they would not at this day think it a great happiness to have been sold for food at a year old, in the manner I prescribe, and thereby have avoided such a perpetual scene of misfortunes, as they have since gone through, by the oppression of landlords, the impossibility of paying rent without money or trade, the want of common sustenance, with neither house nor cloaths to cover them from the inclemencies of the weather, and the most inevitable prospect of intailing the like, or greater miseries, upon their breed for ever.

I profess, in the sincerity of my heart, that I have not the least personal interest in endeavouring to promote this necessary work, having no other motive than the publick good of my country, by advancing our trade, providing for infants, relieving the poor, and giving some pleasure to the rich. I have no children, by which I can propose to get a single penny; the youngest being nine years old, and my wife past child-bearing.

## Questions:

1. Swift asks not to be reminded of certain alternatives to his idea. What are some of these ideas? Why does he mention them?

2. What is ironic about the last sentence in the essay?

3. Why, according to Swift, will the new dish be especially popular with landlords?

4. What girls does Swift offer as suitable sources of food? Why does he say this?

5. What does Swift have to say about Roman Catholics? Is he sincere?

6. What are some targets of this satire?

# Mark Twain

In the passage below, Twain gives his critique of the writing of the American author James Fenimore Cooper (1789-1851). Cooper's *Leatherstocking Tales* describes the adventures of the fictional Native American Natty Bumpo and his fellow frontier-guides.

Twain prefaces his essay with quotes from two professors of literature and the writer Wilkie Collins. All three men complimented Cooper on his style and art.

## Cooper's Literary Offenses

IT SEEMS TO ME that it was far from right for the two professors of English literature and Wilkie Collins to deliver opinions on Cooper's literature without having read some of it. It would have been much more decorous[1] to keep silent and let persons talk who have read Cooper.

Cooper's art has some defects. In one place in *Deerslayer*,[2] and in the restricted space of two-thirds of a page, Cooper has scored 114 offenses against literary art out of a possible 115. It breaks the record.

There are nineteen rules governing literary art in the domain of romantic fiction—some say twenty-two. In *Deerslayer* Cooper violated eighteen of them. These eighteen require:

1. That a tale shall accomplish something and arrive somewhere. But *The Deerslayer* tale accomplishes nothing and arrives in the air.

2. They require that the episodes of a tale shall be necessary parts of the tale, and shall help to develop it. But as *The Deerslayer* tale is not a tale, and accomplishes nothing and arrives nowhere, the episodes have no rightful place in the work, since there was nothing for them to develop.

3. They require that the personages in a tale shall be alive, except in the case of corpses, and that always the reader shall be able to tell the corpses from the others. But this detail has often been overlooked in *The Deerslayer* tale.

4. They require that the personages in a tale, both dead and alive, shall exhibit a sufficient excuse for being there. But this detail also has been overlooked in *The Deerslayer* tale.

[1]decorous–polite and courteous
[2]*Deerslayer*–1841 novel by Cooper.

5. They require that when the personages of a tale deal in conversation, the talk shall sound like human talk, and be talk such as human beings would be likely to talk in the given circumstances, and have a discoverable meaning, also a discoverable purpose, and a show of relevancy, and remain in the neighborhood of the subject in hand, and be interesting to the reader, and help out the tale, and stop when the people cannot think of anything more to say. But this requirement has been ignored from the beginning of *The Deerslayer* tale to the end of it.

6. They require that when the author describes the character of a personage in his tale, the conduct and conversation of that personage shall justify said description. But this law gets little or no attention in *The Deerslayer* tale, as Natty Bumppo's case will amply prove.

7. They require that when a personage talks like an illustrated, gilt-edged, hand-tooled, seven-dollar Friendship's Offering[3] in the beginning of a paragraph, he shall not talk like a Negro minstrel in the end of it. But this rule is flung down and danced upon in *The Deerslayer* tale.

8. They require that crass stupidities shall not be played upon the reader as "the craft of the woodsman, the delicate art of the forest," by either the author or the people in the tale. But this rule is persistently violated in *The Deerslayer* tale.

9. They require that the personages of a tale shall confine themselves to possibilities and let miracles alone; or, if they venture a miracle, the author must so plausibly set it forth as to make it look possible and reasonable. But these rules are not respected in *The Deerslayer* tale.

10. They require that the author shall make the reader feel a deep interest in the personages of his tale and in their fate; and that he shall make the reader love the good people in the tale and hate the bad ones. But the reader of *The Deerslayer* tale dislikes the good people in it, is indifferent to the others, and wishes they would all get drowned together.

11. They require that the characters in a tale shall be so clearly defined that the reader can tell beforehand what each will do in a given emergency. But in *The Deerslayer* tale this rule is vacated.

[3]Friendship's Offering—elaborate prayer

In addition to these large rules there are some little ones. These require that the author shall:

12. Say what he is proposing to say, not merely come near it.

13. Use the right word, not its second cousin.

14. Eschew surplusage.

15. Not omit necessary details.

16. Avoid slovenliness of form.

17. Employ a simple and straightforward style.

18. Use good grammar.

Even these seven are coldly and persistently violated in *The Deerslayer tale*

Cooper's gift in the way of invention was not a rich endowment; but such as it was he liked to work it; he was pleased with the effects, and indeed he did some quite sweet things with it. In his little box of stage-properties he kept six or eight cunning devices, tricks, artifices for his savages and woodsmen to deceive and circumvent each other with, and he was never so happy as when he was working these innocent things and seeing them go. A favorite one was to make a moccasined person tread in the tracks of the moccasined enemy, and thus hide his own trail. Cooper wore out barrels and barrels of moccasins in working that trick. Another stage-property that he pulled out of his box pretty frequently was his broken twig. He prized his broken twig above all the rest of his effects, and worked it the hardest. It is a restful chapter in any book of his when somebody doesn't step on a dry twig and alarm all the reds and whites for two hundred yards around. Every time a Cooper person is in peril, and absolute silence is worth four dollars a minute, he is sure to step on a dry twig. There may be a hundred handier things to step on, but that wouldn't satisfy Cooper. Cooper requires him to turn out and find a dry twig. In fact, *The Leatherstocking Series* ought to have been called *The Broken Twig Series*.

Now in one place he loses some "females"—as he always calls women—on purpose to give Bumppo a chance to show off the delicate art of the forest before the reader. These mislaid people are hunting for a fort. They hear cannon blast, and a cannon-ball presently comes rolling into the wood and stops at their feet. To the females this suggests nothing. The case is very different with the admirable Bumppo. I wish I may never know peace again if he doesn't strike out promptly and follow the track of that cannon-ball across the plain through the dense fog and find the fort. Isn't it a daisy? If Cooper had any real knowledge of Nature's way of doing things, he had a most delicate art in concealing the fact.

For instance: one of his acute Indian experts, Chingachogook (pronounced Chicago, I think), has lost the trail of a person he is tracking through the forest. Apparently that trail is hopelessly lost. Neither you nor I could ever have guessed out the way to find it. It was very different with Chicago. Chicago was not stumped for long. He turned a running stream out of its course, and there, in the slush in its old bed, were that person's moccasin tracks. The current did not wash them away, as it would have done in all other cases—no, even the eternal laws of Nature have to vacate when Cooper wants to put up a delicate job of woodcraft[4] on the reader.

If Cooper had been an observer his inventive faculty would have worked better; not more interestingly, but more rationally, more plausibly. Cooper's eye was splendidly inaccurate. Cooper seldom saw anything correctly. He saw nearly all things as through a glass eye, darkly. Of course a man who cannot see the commonest little everyday matters accurately is working at a disadvantage when he is constructing a "situation."

In *The Deerslayer* tale Cooper has a stream which is fifty feet wide where it flows out of a lake; it presently narrows to twenty as it meanders along for no given reason, and yet when a stream acts like that it ought to be required to explain itself. Fourteen pages later the width of the brook's outlet from the lake has suddenly shrunk thirty feet, and become "the narrowest part of the stream." This shrinkage is not accounted for. The stream has bends in it, a sure indication that it has alluvial[5] banks and cuts them; yet these bends are only thirty and fifty feet long. If Cooper had been a nice and punctilious[6] observer, he would have noticed that the bends were oftener nine hundred feet long than short of it.

Cooper made the exit of that stream fifty feet wide, in the first place, for no particular reason; in the second place, he narrowed it to less than twenty to accommodate some Indians. He bends a "sapling" to the form of an arch over this narrow passage, and conceals six Indians in its foliage. They are "laying" for a settler's scow[7] or ark[8] which is coming up the stream on its way to the lake; it is being hauled against the stiff current by a rope whose stationary end is anchored in the lake; its rate of progress cannot be more than a mile an hour. Cooper describes the ark, but pretty obscurely. In the matter of dimensions "it was little more than a modern canalboat." Let us guess, then, that it was about one hundred and forty feet long. It was of "greater breadth than common." Let us guess, then,

[4]woodcraft—decption
[5]alluvial—deposited or formed by moving water
[6]punctilious—careful
[7]scow—arge, flat-bottomed boat
[8]ark—large, awkward boat

that it was about sixteen feet wide. This leviathan[9] had been prowling down bends which were but a third as long as itself, and scraping between banks where it had only two feet of space to spare on each side. We cannot too much admire this miracle. A low-roofed log dwelling occupies "two-thirds of the ark's length"—a dwelling ninety feet long and sixteen feet wide. The ark is arriving at the stream's exit now, whose width has been reduced to less than twenty feet to accommodate the Indians—say to eighteen. There is a foot to spare on each side of the boat. Did the Indians notice that there was going to be a tight squeeze there? Did they notice that they could make money by climbing down out of that arched sapling and just stepping aboard when the ark scraped by? No, other Indians would have noticed these things, but Cooper's Indians never notice anything. Cooper thinks they are marvelous creatures for noticing, but he was almost always in error about his Indians. There was seldom a sane one among them.

The ark is one hundred and forty feet long; the dwelling is ninety feet long. The idea of the Indians is to drop softly and secretly from the arched sapling to the dwelling as the ark creeps along under it at the rate of a mile an hour, and butcher the family. It will take the ark a minute and a half to pass under. It will take the ninety-foot dwelling a minute to pass under. Now, then, what did the six Indians do? It would take you thirty years to guess, and even then you would have to give it up, I believe. Therefore, I will tell you what the Indians did. Their chief, a person of quite extraordinary intellect for a Cooper Indian, warily watched the canal-boat as it squeezed along under him, and when he had got his calculations lined down to exactly the right shade, he let go and dropped. And missed the house! That is actually what he did. He missed the house, and landed in the stern of the scow. It was not much of a fall, yet it knocked him silly.

There still remained in the roost five Indians. The boat has passed under and is now out of their reach. Let me explain what the five did—you could not be able to reason it out for yourself. No. 1 jumped for the boat, but fell in the water astern of it. Then No. 2 jumped for the boat, but fell in the water still farther astern of it. Then No. 3 jumped for the boat, and fell a good way astern of it. Then No. 4 jumped for the boat, and fell in the water away astern. Then even No. 5 made a jump for the boat—for he was a Cooper Indian. In the matter of intellect, the difference between a Cooper Indian and the Indian that stands in front of the cigar-shop is not spacious. The scow episode is really a sublime burst of invention; but it does not thrill, because the inaccuracy of the details throws a sort of air of fictitiousness and general improbability over it. This comes of Cooper's inadequacy as an observer.

. . . . . .

[9]leviathan–giant

The conversations in the Cooper books have a curious sound in our modern ears. To believe that such talk really ever came out of people's mouths would be to believe that there was *a time* when time was of no value to a person who thought he had something to say; *a time* when it was the custom to spread a two-minute remark out to ten; *a time* when subjects were seldom faithfully stuck to, but the talk wandered all around and arrived nowhere.

Cooper was certainly not a master in the construction of dialogue. Inaccurate observation defeated him here as it defeated him in so many other enterprises of his. He even failed to notice that the man who talks corrupt English six days in the week must and will talk it on the seventh, and can't help himself. In *The Deerslayer* story he lets Deerslayer talk the showiest kind of book-talk sometimes, and at other times the basest of base dialects. For instance, when some one asks him if he has a sweetheart, and if so, where she lives, this is his majestic answer:

> *"She's in the forest—hanging from the boughs of the trees, in a soft rain—in the dew on the open grass—in the clouds that float about in the blue heavens—with the birds that sing in the woods —the sweet springs where I slake my thirst and in all the other glorious gifts that come from God's Providence!"*

And he preceded that, a little before, with this:

> *"It consarns me as all things that touches a fri'nd consarns a fri'nd."*

And this is another of his remarks:

> *"If I was Injin born, now, I might tell of this, or carry in the scalp and boast of the expl'ite afore the whole tribe; Or if my inimy had only been a bear."*

· · · · ·

Cooper's wordsense was singularly dull. When a person has a poor ear for music he will flat and sharp right along without knowing it. He keeps near the tune, but it is not the tune. You perceive what he is intending to say, but you also perceive that he doesn't say it. This is Cooper. He was not a word musician. His ear was satisfied with the approximate word.

I will furnish some circumstantial evidence in support of this charge. My instances are gathered from half a dozen pages of the tale called *Deerslayer*. He uses "verbal" for "oral"; "precision" for "facility"; "necessary" for "predetermined"; "unsophisticated" for "primitive"; "preparation" for "expectancy"; "rebuked" for "subdued"; "precaution" for "caution"; "explain" for " determine"; "mortified" for " disappointed"; "treacherous" for "hostile"; "rejoined" for "remarked"; "situation" for "condition"; "different" for "differing"; "distrusted" for "suspicious";

There have been daring people in the world who claimed that Cooper could write English, but they are all dead now—all dead but Professor Lounsbury. Lounsbury makes the claim that *Deerslayer* is a "pure work of art." Pure, in that connection, means faultless—faultless in all details and language is a detail. If Mr. Lounsbury had only compared Cooper's English with the English which he writes himself—but it is plain that he didn't; and so it is likely that he imagines until this day that Cooper's writing is as clean and compact as his own. Now I feel sure, deep down in my heart, that Cooper wrote about the poorest English that exists in our language, and that the English of *Deerslayer* is the worst that even Cooper ever wrote.

I may be mistaken, but it does seem to me that *The Deerslayer* is not a work of art in any sense.

A work of art? It has no invention; it has no order, system, sequence, or result; it has no lifelikeness, no thrill, no stir, no seeming of reality; its characters are confusedly drawn, and by their acts and words they prove that they are not the sort of people the author claims that they are; its humor is pathetic; its pathos is funny; its conversations are—indescribable; its love-scenes odious; its English a crime against the language.

Counting these out, what is left is Art. I think we must all admit that.

## Questions:

1. Twain provides numbers for the rules that govern literature—one hundred fourteen for literary art, nineteen for romantic fiction. Is he sincere about these numbers, or is he making them up?

2. Why does Twain calculate the measurements of the boat and the width of the river for us? What is he trying to show?

3. What words would you use to describe Twain's tone?

## Essay Question:

What do you think the ultimate purpose of this essay is? Does Twain want mistakes like Cooper's to be corrected, or is he writing to entertain his audience? Compare his purpose to that of one other satirist in this book.

# H. L. Mencken

H.L. Mencken was a newspaper editor and columnist for the Baltimore Sun for thirty years. In his columns, Mencken mocked the faults and foibles of the American people, to whom he referred as the "booboisie" or the "boobus Americanus." In the selection that follows, Mencken begins by attacking the disillusioned Young Intellectuals, who are leaving America to live as expatriates in Europe.

## ON BEING AN AMERICAN

APPARENTLY THERE ARE those who begin to find it disagreeable—nay, impossible. Their anguish fills the Liberal weeklies, and every ship that puts out from New York carries a groaning cargo of them, bound for Paris, London, Munich, Rome and way points—anywhere to escape the great curses and atrocities that make life intolerable for them at home. Let me say at once that I find little to cavil[1] at in their basic complaints. In more than one direction, indeed, I probably go a great deal further than even the Young Intellectuals. It is, for example, one of my firmest and most sacred beliefs, reached after an inquiry extending over a score of years and supported by prayer and meditation, that the government of the United States, in both its legislative arm and its executive arm, is ignorant, incompetent, corrupt, and disgusting—and from this judgment I except no more than twenty living lawmakers and no more than twenty executioners of their laws. It is a belief no less piously cherished that the administration of justice in the Republic is stupid, dishonest, and against all reason and equity—and from this judgment I except no more than thirty judges, including two upon the bench of the Supreme Court of the United States. It is another that the foreign policy of the United States—its habitual manner of dealing with other nations, whether friend or foe—is hypocritical, knavish,[2] and dishonorable—and from this judgment I consent to no exceptions whatever, either recent or long past. And it is my fourth (and, to avoid too depressing a bill, final) conviction that the American people, taking one with another, constitute the most timorous, sniveling, poltroonish, ignominious mob of serfs and goose-steppers ever gathered under one flag in

[1]cavil–complain
[2]knavish–deceitful, lowdown

Christendom since the end of the Middle Ages, and that they grow more timorous, more sniveling, more poltroonish, more ignominious every day.

Yet I remain on the dock, wrapped in the flag, when the Young Intellectuals set sail. Yet here I stand, unshaken and undespairing, a loyal and devoted Americano, even a chauvinist,[3] paying taxes without complaint, obeying all laws that are physiologically obeyable, accepting all the searching duties and responsibilities of citizenship unprotestingly, investing the sparse benefits of my miserable toil in the obligations of the nation, avoiding all commerce with men sworn to overthrow the government, contributing my mite toward the glory of the national arts and sciences, enriching and embellishing the native language, spurning all lures (and even all invitations) to get out and stay out—here am I, a bachelor of easy means, forty-two years old, unhampered by debts or issue, able to go wherever I please, and to stay as long as I please—here am I, contentedly and even smugly basking beneath the Stars and Stripes, a better citizen, I daresay, than thousands who put the Hon. Warren Gamaliel Harding[4] beside Friedrich Barbarossa[5] and Charlemagne,[6] and hold the Supreme Court to be directly inspired by the Holy Spirit, and belong ardently to every Rotary Club, Ku Klux Klan, and Anti-Saloon League, and choke with emotion when the band plays "The Star-Spangled Banner," and believe with the faith of little children that one of Our Boys, taken at random, could dispose in a fair fight of ten Englishmen, twenty Germans, thirty Frogs,[7] forty Wops,[8] fifty Japs, or a hundred Bolsheviki.[9]

Well, then, why am I still here? Why am I so complacent (perhaps even to the point of offensiveness), so free from bile, so little fretting and indignant, so curiously happy? Why did I answer only with a few academic "Hear, Hears" when Henry James,[10] Ezra Pound, Harold Stearns and the emigres of Greenwich Village issued their successive calls to the corn-fed intelligentsia to flee the shambles, escape to fairer lands, throw off the curse forever? The answer, of course, is to be sought in the nature of happiness, which tempts to metaphysics. But let me keep upon the ground. To me, at least (and I can only follow my own nose), happiness

[3]chauvinist—militant patriot
[4]Warren Gameliel Harding—twenty-ninth president of the US; members of his administration were involved in illegal activity
[5]Friedrich Barbarossa—Emperor Frederick I of Germany, a famous political leader
[6]Charlemagne—King of the Franks and Holy Roman Emperor in the ninth century; one of the most skilled kings in Western history
[7]Frogs—derogatory name for the French
[8]Wops—derogatory name for the Italians
[9]Bolsheviki—derogatory name for Russian Communists
[10]Henry James, Ezra Pound, Harold Stearns—James and Pound were writers who chose to live in Europe; Stearns was the editor of a publication criticizing the US government.

presents itself in an aspect that is tripartite.[11] To be happy (reducing the thing to its elementals) I must be:

a.  Well-fed, unhounded by sordid cares, at ease in Zion.[12]
b.  Full of a comfortable feeling of superiority to the masses of my fellowmen.
c.  Delicately and unceasingly amused according to my taste.

It is my contention that, if this definition be accepted, there is no country on the face of the earth wherein a man roughly constituted as I am—a man of my general weaknesses, vanities, appetites, prejudices, and aversions—can be so happy, or even one-half so happy, as he can be in these free and independent states. Going further, I lay down the proposition that it is a sheer physical impossibility for such a man to live in These States and not be happy—that it is as impossible to him as it would be to a schoolboy to weep over the burning down of his school-house. If he says that he isn't happy here, then he either lies or is insane. Here the business of getting a living, particularly since the war brought the loot of all Europe to the national strong-box, is enormously easier than it is in any other Christian land—so easy, in fact, that an educated man who fails at it must actually make deliberate efforts to that end. Here the general average of intelligence, of knowledge, of competence, of integrity, of self-respect, of honor is so low that any man who knows his trade, does not fear ghosts, has read fifty good books, and practices the common decencies stands out as brilliantly as a wart on a bald head, and is thrown willy-nilly into a meager and exclusive aristocracy. And here, more than anywhere else that I know of or have heard of, the daily panorama of human existence, of private and communal folly—the unending procession of governmental extortions and chicaneries,[13] of commercial brigandages[14] and throat-slittings, of theological buffooneries,[15] or aesthetic ribaldries,[16] of legal swindles and harlotries, of miscellaneous rogueries, villainies, imbecilities, grotesqueries, and extravagances—is so inordinately[17] gross and preposterous, so perfectly brought up to the highest conceivable amperage, so steadily enriched with an almost fabulous daring and originality, that only the man who was born with a petrified diaphragm can fail to laugh himself to sleep every night, and to awake every morning with all the eager, unflagging expectation of a Sunday-school superintendent touring the Paris peep-shows.

· · · · ·

[11]tripartite—in three parts
[12]Zion—In the Old Testament, the homeland of the Israelites; symbolically, heaven or paradise
[13]chicaneries—deceptions; swindles
[14]brigandages—thefts
[15]buffooneries—ridiculous displays
[16]ribaldries—obscenities
[17]inordinately—overabundantly

2

All of which may be boiled down to this: that the United States is essentially a commonwealth of third-rate men—that distinction is easy here because the general level of culture, of information, of taste and judgment, of ordinary competence is so low. No sane man, employing an American plumber to repair a leaky drain, would expect him to do it at the first trial, and in precisely the same way no sane man, observing an American Secretary of State in negotiation with Englishmen and Japs, would expect him to come off better than second best. Third-rate men, of course, exist in all countries, but it is only here that they are in full control of the state, and with it of all the national standards. The land was peopled, not by the hardy adventurers of legend, but simply by incompetents who could not get on at home, and the lavishness of nature that they found here, the vast ease with which they could get livings, confirmed and augmented their native incompetence. No American colonist, even in the worst days of the Indian wars, ever had to face such hardships as ground down the peasants of Central Europe during the Hundred Years War, nor even such hardships as oppressed the English lower classes during the century before the Reform Bill of 1832. In most of the colonies, indeed, he seldom saw any Indians at all: the one thing that made life difficult for him was his congenital dunderheadedness. The winning of the West, so rhetorically celebrated in American romance, cost the lives of fewer men than the single battle of Tannenberg,[18] and the victory was much easier and surer. The immigrants who have come in since those early days have been, if anything, of even lower grade than their forerunners. The old notion that the United States is peopled by the offspring of brave, idealistic and liberty loving minorities, who revolted against injustice and bigotry at home—this notion is fast succumbing to the alarmed study that has been given of late to the immigration of recent years. The truth is that the majority of non-Anglo-Saxon immigrants since the Revolution, like the majority of Anglo-Saxon immigrants before the Revolution, have been, not the superior men of their native lands, but the botched and unfit: Irishmen starving to death in Ireland, Germans unable to weather the Sturm and Drang of the post-Napoleonic reorganization, Italians weed-grown on exhausted soil, Scandinavians run to all bone and no brain, Jews too incompetent to swindle even the barbarous peasants of Russia, Poland and Romania. Here and there among the immigrants, of course, there may be a bravo, or even a superman

[18]Tannenberg–site of a 1914 battle between the Germans and Russians

e.g., the ancestors of Volstead,[19] Ponzi,[20] Jack Dempsey,[21] Schwab,[22] Daugherty,[23] Debs,[24] Pershing[25]—but the average newcomer is, and always has been, simply a poor fish.

[19]Volstead–Member of Congress responsible for the act that prohibited
    the sale of alcohol
[20]Ponzi–Charles Ponzi, who came up with a financial plan that backfired
    and left many Americans bankrupt
[21]Jack Dempsey–American heavyweight boxer
[22]Schwab–owner of Bethlehem Steel Corporation
[23]Daughtery–Harry Daugherty, U.S. Attorney General accused of trying
    to defraud the U.S. government
[24]Debs–Eugene Debs, a political leader and candidate for the presidency
[25]Pershing–General John Joseph ("Blackjack") Pershing, a major
    military leader during World War I

## Questions:

1. Why does Mencken choose to stay in America? Do you think he is serious?

2. Are Mencken's sentences long or short? Why does he phrase his language this way?

3. Is the tone of this satire gentle or harsh?

## Essay Question:

What is Mencken's theory about why people chose to immigrate to America? Do you agree or disagree? Explain your own ideas about whether immigration strengthens character or weakens it.

# Mike Royko

Royko (1932-1997) was a lifetime resident of Chicago and a writer for both of the city's major newspapers, the *Sun-Times* and the *Tribune*. The following editorial entitled *"Let's Update City's Image,"* written by Mike Royko on October 27, 1967 is reprinted by permission from the ©*Chicago Sun-Times*.

## *Let's Update City's Image*

Chicago needs a new city seal.

The old seal—with its themes of a garden-city, an Indian, an early settler, and a cherub—is out of date.

We need a seal that captures the modern spirit of Chicago.

Therefore, I am launching a city-wide contest for a new seal. It is open to all doodlers, sketchers, and serious and amateur artists.

Below you see an example of what I have in mind.

The clasped hands represent the true spirit of Chicago friendship—especially when the concrete is being poured.

Under the clasped hands, you see the happy city worker clearing the way for still another new improvement.

And the exploding car in the right-hand corner represents the festive spirit of Chicago.

Once we have a new city seal, we will need a new city motto. That I have provided.

The old one is *Urbs in Horto* (City in a Garden).

The invention of the concrete mixer has made the old motto meaningless.

The new motto—*Ubi Est Mea*—means "Where's Mine?"

The phrase "Where's Mine?" can be heard wherever improvements for the city are being planned.

It is the watchword of the new Chicago, the cry of the money brigade, the chant of the city of the big wallet.

The sketch in today's column is merely a rough suggestion, an idea, a guideline, for what your entries might contain.

Except for the city motto, all artists are encouraged to draw upon their imagination.

Some may choose to portray something that brings in the spirit of the new Lake Michigan—an oil slick, a dead alewife,[1] a growling germ.

Others may wish to portray the spirit of urban renewal. Or the theme of the new Chicago's air.

The capacity of our different racial groups to live together in peace and good will might be an inspiration.

It is even possible that someone might want to include Mayor Daley,[2] who discovered Chicago, in a city seal.

The rules for this contest are simple.

Entries should be drawn large enough to be reproduced. Make them about the size of an alderman's wallet—about eight inches across or bigger.

Use the suggested slogan—"Where's Mine?"

As entries are received, I will show them in this column.

Final judging will be done by a panel of distinguished Chicagoans, none of whom has ever been convicted of a heinous crime, held public office, appeared in a society page story, or served on one of the mayor's committees.

The winner and the runners-up will receive many wonderful prizes. The prize list has not been completed, but it includes:

* An all-expense-paid fishing trip in the south end of Lake Michigan.
* Dinner for four at the Red Star Inn,[3] if it isn't gone by then.
* A free chest X-ray at the hospital of your choice.
* A choice in remedial English—or basic English—for the Chicago public school student of your choice.
* A picture of your old neighborhood—if you can find it under the concrete.

---

[1]alewife–herring-like fish
[2]Mayor Daley–Richard J. Daley, Mayor from 1955-1976; Royko wrote a book, *Boss*, describing Daley's violence and corruption
[3]Red Star Inn–famous Chicago landmark; since torn down

**Questions:**

1. What images would accurately represent the new Chicago, according to Royko?

2. What are some of the "prizes" for winning entries? What is the writer actually criticizing when he mentions these prizes?

3. What person or people is Royko targeting in this satire?

4. How can you tell this is satire?


**Research Opportunity:**

Pick one of the items below, and explain why Mike Royko wrote about it.

- Democratic National Convention of 1968
- Curse of the Cubs
- Chicago Seven
- Picasso

# Insightful and Reader-Friendly, Yet Affordable

Prestwick House Literary Touchstone Editions–
The Editions By Which All Others May Be Judged

Every Prestwick House Literary Touchstone Edition™ is enhanced with Reading Pointers for Sharper Insight to improve comprehension and provide insights that will help students recognize key themes, symbols, and plot complexities. In addition, each title includes a Glossary of the more difficult words and concepts.

For the Shakespeare titles, along with the Reading Pointers and Glossary, we include margin notes and eleven strategies to understanding the language of Shakespeare.

*Special Introductory Educator's Discount – At Least 50% Off*

New titles are constantly being added; call or visit our website for current listing.

| | | Retail Price | Intro. Discount |
|---|---|---|---|
| 200102 | **Red Badge of Courage, The** | ~~$3.99~~ | $1.99 |
| 200163 | **Romeo and Juliet** | ~~$3.99~~ | $1.99 |
| 200074 | **Heart of Darkness** | ~~$3.99~~ | $1.99 |
| 200079 | **Narrative of the Life of Frederick Douglass** | ~~$3.99~~ | $1.99 |
| 200125 | **Macbeth** | ~~$3.99~~ | $1.99 |
| 200053 | **Adventures of Huckleberry Finn, The** | ~~$4.99~~ | $2.49 |
| 200081 | **Midsummer Night's Dream, A** | ~~$3.99~~ | $1.99 |
| 200179 | **Christmas Carol, A** | ~~$3.99~~ | $1.99 |
| 200150 | **Call of the Wild, The** | ~~$3.99~~ | $1.99 |
| 200190 | **Dr. Jekyll and Mr. Hyde** | ~~$3.99~~ | $1.99 |
| 200141 | **Awakening, The** | ~~$3.99~~ | $1.99 |
| 200147 | **Importance of Being Earnest, The** | ~~$3.99~~ | $1.99 |
| 200166 | **Ethan Frome** | ~~$3.99~~ | $1.99 |
| 200146 | **Julius Caesar** | ~~$3.99~~ | $1.99 |
| 200095 | **Othello** | ~~$3.99~~ | $1.99 |
| 200091 | **Hamlet** | ~~$3.99~~ | $1.99 |
| 200231 | **Taming of the Shrew, The** | ~~$3.99~~ | $1.99 |
| 200133 | **Metamorphosis, The** | ~~$3.99~~ | $1.99 |

# Give Your Students Editions They'll Really Read!

## Prestwick House Spotlight Editions™

New titles are constantly being added, call or visit our website for current listing.

Prestwick House's new *Spotlight Editions*™ are thoughtful adaptations, written on a tenth-grade level, that keep all of the symbolism, conflict, and character development of the original. We've enriched our adaptations with sidebar commentary and guided reading questions to help your students read carefully and intelligently.

Writing and research opportunities, topics for discussion, and a teacher's guide make studying and teaching the classics an enriching experience for everyone.

### A Christmas Carol
200979 ............Single Copy ...................................**$5.95**
300190 ...........30 Books & Teachers Guide......**$149.99**

### The Scarlet Letter
200187 ............Single Copy ...................................**$5.95**
300979 ...........30 Books & Teachers Guide......**$149.99**

### The Call of the Wild
200710 ...........Single Copy ...................................**$5.95**
300150 ...........30 Books & Teachers Guide......**$149.99**

### The Awakening
201794 ...........Single Copy ...................................**$5.95**
300104 ...........30 Books & Teachers Guide......**$149.99**

# PRESTWICK HOUSE, INC.
## "Everything for the English Classroom!"

Prestwick House, Inc. • P.O. Box 658, Clayton, DE 19938
Phone (800) 932-4593 • Fax (888) 718-9333 • www.prestwickhouse.com